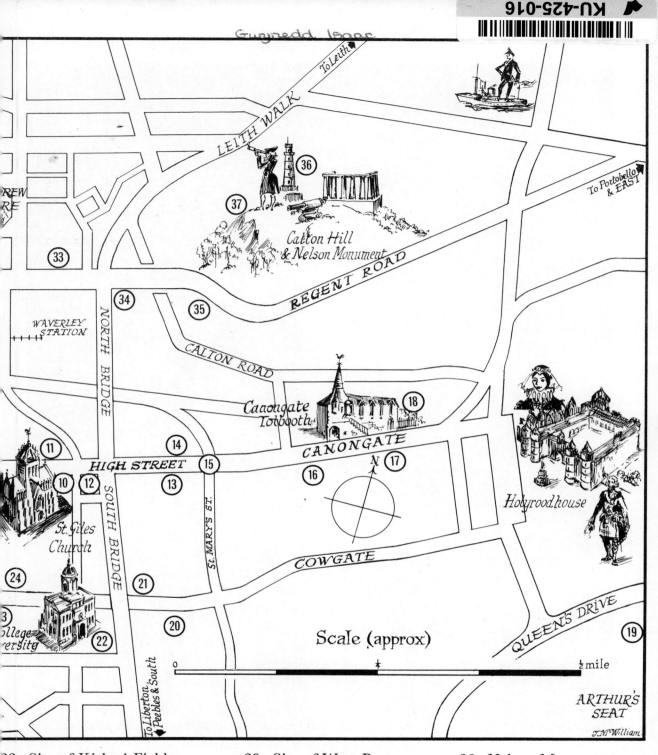

22. Site of Kirk o' Field
23. Royal Scottish Museum
24. Heriot-Watt College
25. Greyfriars Church
26. Magdalen Chapel
27. Edinburgh Public Library
28. Flodden Wall

29. Site of West Port
30. St Cuthbert's Church
31. Floral Clock
32. Art Galleries
33. Register House
34. General Post Office
35. St Andrew's House

36. Nelson Monument
37. City Observatory
38. Museum of Antiquities
39. St Andrew's Church
40. Assembly Rooms
41. Adam Architecture
42. Dean Bridge

THE SEARCHLIGHT TATTOO AT THE CASTLE

EDINBURGH

from the Earliest Times to the Present Day

J. B. BARCLAY

WITH NINE MAPS, AND TWO HUNDRED AND
TWENTY ILLUSTRATIONS FROM CONTEMPORARY
PRINTS AND PHOTOGRAPHS AND FROM DRAW-
INGS BY J. McWILLIAM

ADAM AND CHARLES BLACK

LONDON

A Companion Book

LONDON

from the Earliest Times to the Present Day

by JOHN HAYES

ACKNOWLEDGEMENTS

The maps and many of the drawings in this book are by J. McWilliam. The cover design, also by J. McWilliam, shows on the front (clockwise, beginning left): John Napier, John Knox, Mary Queen of Scots, Bonnie Prince Charlie, Queen Margaret, Agricola, an Old Town Guard, a City Merchant; and on the back: a Member of the Royal Company of Archers, a student, Dr. Simpson, Lord Newton, a Highlander, Robert Burns, Clarinda, Robert Louis Stevenson, Sir Walter Scott.

The illustrations on pages 21 (b) and 47 (c) are reproduced by gracious permission of Her Majesty the Queen.

Grateful acknowledgement is made to the following for their permission to reproduce drawings and photographs: *The Scotsman*, pages 64 (b), 69 (a), 72 (b), 76 (b), 81 (b), 86 (b), 87 (b), 89 (a), 94 (b), 95 (b), 96 (b), 97 (a and b), 98 (a), 99 (a, b and c), 100 (a), 101 (a and b), 102 (b), 103 (a, b and c), 104 (b), 105 (a and b), 107 (a and b), 108 (a and c); Scottish National Buildings Record, 22 (a and b), 23 (a and b), 32 (c), 34 (b), 36 (a), 49 (a and c), 58 (a), 60 (b), 62 (a and b), 63 (a), 73 (a), 83 (b), 85 (a and c), 90 (b), 92 (c), 100 (c); Edinburgh Public Library, 29 (a), 41 (a), 50 (a), 51 (a), 52 (a and b), 53 (b), 54 (a and b), 56 (a), 61 (b), 66 (b), 69 (b), 70 (b), 74 (b and c), 76 (a), 78 (c), 80 (a), 81 (a), 84 (b), 86 (a), 87 (c), 89 (b), 91 (b); Crown Copyrights by permission of the Ministry of Works, 9 (a), 43 (b), 50 (b), 108 (b); Robin Hill, 33 (a), 65 (c), 106 (a, b and c); Bodleian Library, 9 (b), 28 (a); The Dean and Chapter of Westminster, 10 (b); *The Book of the Old Edinburgh Club*, 12 (b), 53 (c); Pitkin Pictorials Ltd., 26 (b); British Travel and Holidays Association, frontispiece, 31, 90 (b); *The Edinburgh Evening News and Dispatch*, 45 (b); Paul Shillabeer, 90 (a); Aerofilms Ltd., 94 (a); Ministry of Aviation, 98 (b); Scottish Tourist Board, 102 (a); Ferranti Ltd., 60 (a); B.B.C. and Alan Sorrell, 16 (b); the City of Edinburgh, 83 (a); the Bank of Scotland, 100 (b).

THE CITY OF EDINBURGH FROM THE CALTON HILL.
Princes Street is in the centre

CONTENTS

THE MONUMENT ON CALTON HILL to Scots
killed in the Napoleonic Wars

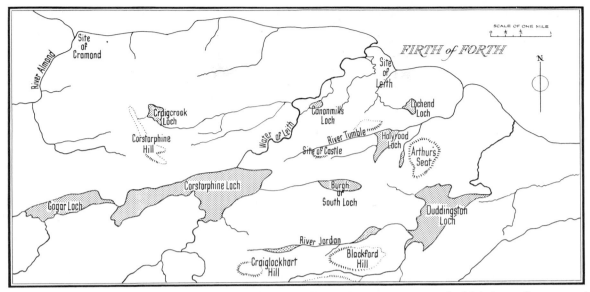

THE SITE OF EDINBURGH IN ANCIENT TIMES had many lochs and streams, most of which have disappeared

1. EDINBURGH UP TO THE ELEVENTH CENTURY

The oldest name of the city of Edinburgh is Dunedin, which probably means the dun or fortress of the district of Edin. *Dun* translated into Anglo-Saxon is *burgh*. So Dun-edin becomes Edin-burgh.

In later times, when the settlers in New Zealand wished to name their new city after the capital of Scotland they chose the older name Dunedin.

The dark-age people of the dun lived on what is now called the Castle rock, but similar peoples inhabited the other hills around.

On Arthur's Seat there are remains of hut circles, cultivation terraces and enclosures. The Castle rock, however, is the only hill which has been inhabited throughout history.

The Romans passed through the Edinburgh area. They left remains of their fort and port at the suburb of Cramond, at the mouth of the River Almond. Where they crossed the River Esk there are remains of villas. The estuary of the Forth they called Bodotria.

THE EARLY INHABITANTS cultivated the hills in and around Edinburgh

5

ROMAN ARMIES kept coming and going from the port and fort of Cramond

When the Romans left, the native Celtic peoples (whom the Roman writer Ptolemy called Votadini) grew more powerful. The heroic tales tell of chosen warriors who lived at the court of Edinburgh, the stronghold on the hill, drinking mead from golden vessels, wearing rich clothing, and riding fine horses.

The fortress was built mainly of wood. The great hall, where the feasting took place, was surrounded by smaller rooms. Nearby the Celtic peoples grew their crops and grazed their cattle.

These people were conquered by the Angles who made Edinburgh one of the chief centres of Northumbria. The Angles, in turn, surrendered the fortress to the Scots under King Indulph in the tenth century. Many of the Gaelic names of the neighbourhood date from this time.

When the Norman immigrants came, they saw how important the rock of Edinburgh was and renamed the fortress *Castrum Puellarum*, or Maidens' Castle.

The rock was an excellent place of defence. It had been a volcano of crag and tail formation. It was steep on three sides but the fourth had a hollow between the crag and the tail. It was large enough to hold many people and strong enough to ensure their defence.

  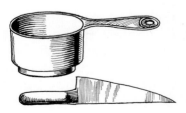

ROMAN VESSELS AND A KNIFE
found near Edinburgh

The whole neighbourhood was forest, loch and stream. Only Duddingston Loch and Lochend Loch are still there today. Corstorphine, Canonmills, Craigcrook, Holyrood, Burgh Lochs and a few smaller sheets of water have disappeared. Many of the streams have been diverted into culverts and their names forgotten.

The principal forest was Drumsheugh. It stretched right round the Castle to Holyrood and beyond. It was the favourite hunting ground of later kings, and deer and other animals roamed freely there.

ST CUTHBERT PREACHED in what is now Princes Street Gardens. The first church was built about the seventh century

The early people took rushes from the marshes to thatch their huts. In the forests they caught animals, eating their flesh and using their skins as clothing.

The early Celtic tribes were Christian, and were probably converted to Christianity by the early missionaries of the Culdee or Columban church. Inchcolm in the Firth of Forth is the island of Columba. St Ninian visited Lothian and St Cuthbert founded an early church whose traditions survive today.

A little later another church was founded and dedicated to St Giles. It was not, however, till the eleventh century that the Roman church was finally established in Edinburgh.

THE COMMON SEAL OF EDINBURGH on which St Giles is seen

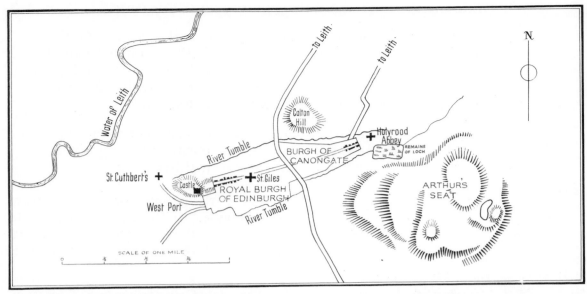

THE ROYAL BURGH OF EDINBURGH IN THE THIRTEENTH CENTURY stretched down the Castlehill. The Burgh of Canongate stretched uphill

2. EDINBURGH UP TO THE THIRTEENTH CENTURY

The real beginnings of modern Edinburgh seem to date from the time of Margaret. She was an English princess who had been educated in Hungary and had fled to Scotland with some of her family at the time of the Norman Conquest of England. She married Malcolm, the King of Scotland, whose nickname was *Canmore*, or Big Head.

Margaret, who was made a saint after her death, lived in the Castle and brought to her rather bleak surroundings some of the culture and civilisation she had learned abroad. She died in the Castle in 1093 but her sons carried on her good works.

QUEEN MARGARET IS LED TO HER CHAPEL on the Castle rock

While the Castle was being attacked by Donald Bane, Malcolm's brother, her body was secretly taken from it and buried across the Forth at Dunfermline. The crossing is known today as Queensferry.

At this time there must have been the beginnings of a town near the Castle. We know this from references in royal charters granted to other towns. The charters say that the citizens of these new towns were to obtain the same liberties and customs in law and property, buying and selling, as the burgesses of Edinburgh.

The town itself must have grown up on an almost vacant site, a bow-shot distance from the Castle. Some of the inhabitants worked the land and others worked at trades and crafts.

There were many early disputes between neighbours about cattle, sheep, pigs and fowls. The *Laws of the Four Burghs*, one of the earliest codes of civil law in existence, devotes a large part to agricultural matters. Edinburgh was one of the four burghs and was, like other burghs, established for trading purposes.

THE CHANCEL ARCH OF MARGARET'S CHAPEL. The flowers on the present-day table are placed there each week by ladies called Margaret

The burgesses of Edinburgh kept their privileges for the next seven hundred years. The city had full powers over the sale in the markets of such things as bread, ale and cloth. A toll or tax, known as petty custom, had to be paid on all articles brought into the market, and a great custom was paid on all goods exported.

Queen Margaret encouraged merchants to come from foreign places with cloths of many colours, ornaments, precious metals and other luxuries.

The officer responsible for collecting the royal revenue from the burgh had the Latin title of *prepositus*, which gradually changed into *provost*. In time the word came to be used for the chief magistrate of the burgh.

LEAVES FROM THE GOSPEL BELONGING TO MARGARET

The names of the inhabitants of this early period include English, Dutch or Flemish and French names. Some of the English may have fled from the Norman invasions. The kings of Scotland encouraged settlers who could help to increase the business and trade of their towns.

The town grew up round a broad street known as the High Street which served as a market-place. Each burgess lived in his own enclosure or close which included his house and his garden. When, centuries later, the ground of the enclosures was built on to provide more accommodation the word *close* came to mean the lane leading to the various parts of the property.

THE STONE OF SCONE, on which the Kings of Scotland were crowned, was carried off by Edward I and is now in the base of the Coronation Chair at Westminster

THE HIGH TABLE IN A NOBLEMAN'S CASTLE

The early houses were built of wood which probably came from the common land of the city or Burgh Muir. Many had mud or plaster filling between the wooden uprights. They were built with their gables facing the street, and were generally whitewashed or coloured.

The burgesses paid a rent for their property but they did not have to perform any feudal service as in England. Edinburgh was a royal burgh and paid a grant of money to the king. The date of its original charter is unknown.

THE CITIZENS GRAZED THEIR CATTLE OUTSIDE THE WALL

The town was protected by a wall. Early documents mention at least two gates. The Netherbow, the eastern gate, was about half-way along the present Royal Mile, between the Castle and the Abbey. The West Port was near the Castle. The royal burgh was a garden city built on the ridge and spread over a little more than 100 acres.

In the thirteenth century came the friars. The Blackfriars established themselves at the east end of the town and the Greyfriars found a site later at the west. Between was the Kirk o' Field which was later to play a tragic part in Scottish history.

IN THE BROAD STREET OF THE ROYAL BURGH
people did business and met their friends

The Blackfriars are now remembered by a street name. On the site of the Greyfriars monastery is the Kirk of the Greyfriars, about which more will be told later. Kirk o' Field has given place to the Old College of the University of Edinburgh.

At the far end of the ridge leading from the Castle is the Abbey and Palace of Holyrood. In 1128 King David founded the abbey of Augustinian monks at Holyrood. The monks had previously lived in his Castle.

Legends are often attached to the foundation of abbeys and Holyrood Abbey is no exception. It is said that the king and his court hunted after mass on the feast of the Exaltation of the Cross, even though advised by his confessor not to do so.

THE FRIARS were the preachers and teachers of the Middle Ages

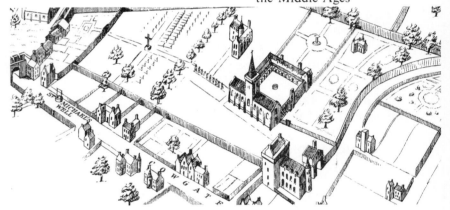

RESTORATION OF THE CHURCH OF THE BLACKFRIARS

RUINS OF KIRK O' FIELD AND OLD GATEWAY

In the forest the king became separated from his companions and was unhorsed by a great stag. A cross held between the antlers made the stag vanish as suddenly as it had come. At night David dreamed that he heard a voice calling him to found an abbey of the holy cross. He brought workmen from France and the Abbey of the Holy Rude (cross) was begun. The stag with its cross appears on the badge of the Canongate. (See page 73.)

Soon houses of the patrons and lay members of the monastery grew round the abbey into a town called Canongate, under the abbot of Holyroodhouse. In time, as the royal burgh of Edinburgh stretched down the slope from the Castle, the burgh of Canongate stretched up the hill to meet at the Netherbow gate of the city.

When the king founded the abbey he gave it and the town beside it many privileges. These included freedom of trade in his royal burgh of Edinburgh, mills on the Water of Leith at Dean and Canonmills and other lands, such as the Barony of Broughton, in and near the present city.

THE ABBEY OF HOLYROOD looked something like this when it was complete

THE SEAL OF THE ABBEY shows a church with a crown tower

CANONMILLS LOCH AND MILLS existed till the nineteenth century

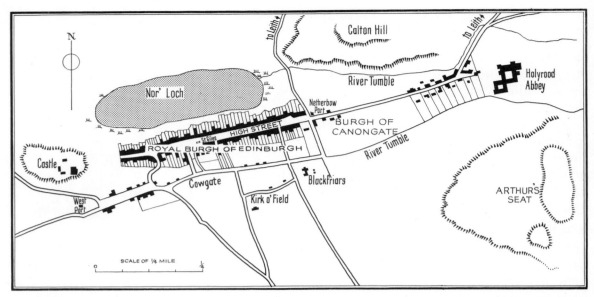

EDINBURGH IN THE FOURTEENTH CENTURY added a new street to the south, Cowgate, which led to the pastures

3. EDINBURGH UP TO THE FIFTEENTH CENTURY

WAR WITH ENGLAND

A TRON WAS A GREAT BEAM AT WHICH GOODS WERE WEIGHED. The Tron Church was built at the place where the Tron stood

By the fourteenth century Edinburgh was becoming more important. Gradually during the reigns of the Stuart kings, Edinburgh came to be regarded as the chief burgh of Scotland. The Stuarts are called after Robert the Steward who became Robert II in 1371.

By the time of James II it was recognised as the capital, and the Abbey of Holyrood became the scene of coronations, royal weddings and other ceremonies. Coronations were previously held at Scone where the Stone of Destiny was kept. The stone is now part of the Coronation Chair in Westminster Abbey. (See picture, page 10.)

Trade was expanding. A new weigh-house or tron was built in the High Street. The king also gave ground for a new tolbooth to be used for the administration of the city as well as a prison and place of justice. It had a bell to summon the citizens to meetings.

14

The city had obtained a new charter in 1329 and the population had increased sufficiently to need a new street, the Cowgate, built in what was the valley of the little River Tumble.

The fourteenth century was a period of strife. The Wars of Scottish Independence were not yet over. The Battle of Bannockburn was not fought till 1314. English troops occupied the castles. Edward I, who was nicknamed the Hammer of the Scots, had carried off Scottish treasures to England.

There is a famous story of how Sir Thomas Randolph, Earl of Moray, was shown a path up the steep Castle rock. A party of thirty men was secretly led up this path, scaled the walls and captured the Castle for Bruce.

When Robert the Bruce became king he ordered the buildings on the Castle rock to be levelled to the ground so that no enemy would ever use the Castle again. He left only one building, the chapel of Queen Margaret, and this survives today, the oldest religious building still used in Edinburgh. (See the illustration on page 9.)

ROBERT THE BRUCE who won Scottish independence granted a new charter to the city in 1329

When David II returned to Scotland after he was released from captivity in England, he began to reconstruct the Castle and build his great tower in 1368. The oldest parts of the present castle date from this time.

David's tower lasted for about 200 years.

DAVID'S TOWER is seen in the foreground of this old drawing of the Castle

Its remains can be seen inside the Half-Moon Battery which was built after the Castle surrendered in 1573.

Despite its strong castle, Edinburgh was not free from attacks by the English kings who had many quarrels with the Scots. It was also attacked by Scottish nobles who struggled for power, especially during the regencies for the child kings.

THE CROWN OR LANTERN OF ST GILES was built about 1500 and is the oldest visible masonry. Although it no longer has a clock-face the bells still chime the quarters

The town and church of St Giles were burnt during the invasion by Richard II in 1385, but the Castle was not taken. Henry IV attacked the Castle in 1400 but he was driven off, mainly because of bad weather and lack of provisions for his troops. Henry VIII sent an army in 1544 and burnt the town together with the Abbey and Palace, but the Castle again stood firm.

In 1481 the king, James III, was held prisoner in his own Castle by some of his nobles. He was not released till the King of England sent the Duke of Gloucester with an armed force to Edinburgh.

A release was peaceably arranged and the citizens of Edinburgh paid the English king for his help. In return they received an important charter in 1482, which increased their privileges.

The royal charter of 1329 had granted Edinburgh the port of Leith, in exchange for an annual rental. The port, probably already in existence, was situated where the Water of Leith entered the Firth of Forth. It was the nearest convenient place to make a harbour to enable Edinburgh to carry on the import and export trade of a royal burgh. It was situated where the street called the Shore is today.

THE GREAT CANNON MONS MEG is escorted from the Castle to a siege. It could fire stone balls weighing 5 cwt nearly $1\frac{3}{4}$ miles

Many of the merchants became very wealthy. They traded in wool, cloth, hides and fish. Pearls were also exported. Ships sailed to the Low Countries, to the Baltic, to France, and even farther south. They returned with silks, velvets, wines and luxuries.

The magistrates had the right to all the customs at Leith and they controlled all the roads leading there.

WEALTHY MERCHANTS BROUGHT THEIR SHIPS TO LEITH

By the new charter of 1482 the provost and bailies became sheriffs within their own territories, with power to impose sentences of death, imprisonment and other punishments. This greatly increased their power.

The merchant guilds were formed in the thirteenth century and played a large part in the government of the burgh. The merchant burgesses ruled the city till 1469 when the town council became a corporation which chose its own members.

The crafts also organised themselves. The craftsmen did not like to be considered inferior to the merchants, with whom they often disagreed. Their position was improved when they were recognised by the town council.

EDINBURGH ABOUT 1450. Note the wall, Netherbow gate, Nor' Loch and on the left the valley of Cowgate

WEAVERS

By the end of the fifteenth century there were in Edinburgh incorporations or societies of cordiners (shoemakers), hatmakers, weavers, hammermen (blacksmiths, pewterers, locksmiths, lorimers or leather-workers, saddlers, cutlers, shearsmiths and armourers), skinners, fleshers (butchers), coopers, wrights and masons, waulkers (fullers), tailors, barbers and surgeons, baxters (bakers) and candlemakers.

SHOEMAKERS

HAMMERMEN

BAKERS

BUTCHERS

THE BADGES OF THE EDINBURGH INCORPORATIONS AND SOCIETIES

The crafts controlled the training of their apprentices and looked after their poor. Many crafts erected and supported altars in St Giles' Church and in other religious institutions of the burgh. By the charter of 1482 the craftsmen of Edinburgh received their famous flag, known as the Blue Blanket, which was long used as a rallying point in any dispute.

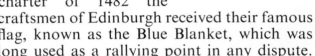

TAILORS

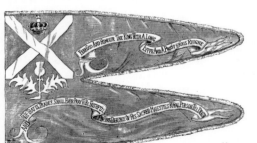

THE "BLUE BLANKET" FLAG OF THE CRAFTSMEN

Craftsmen worked much longer hours in the fifteenth century. We are told that masons employed in enlarging St Giles' began at five o'clock in the morning in summer and continued till seven o'clock at night. They stopped for two hours at eleven o'clock for dinner and had two half-hour breaks for what we might call breakfast and tea. Wages were low and there was much poverty.

HOUSES AND PEOPLE

Houses were still built mainly of wood, with thatched roofs. The wood probably came from the Burgh Muir which stretched south and east of the burgh, roughly where the districts of Newington, Marchmont, Morningside and Merchiston are today.

Strict rules were made which did not allow anyone to carry any light or lighted material from house to house except in a lantern. Citizens had also to keep twenty-foot-long ladders for public use, and iron cleeks to pull down houses or roofs which caught fire.

There were still no great town houses for the nobles or the wealthy, although towards the end of this period they were beginning to be built in the Cowgate. The nobility lived in their castles and towers outside the town.

Nobles who visited the city to attend the court or parliament stayed in the hostelries or inns, or in the guest-houses of the monastery of Holyrood or of the convents of the friars.

AT THE INN the guest gives his horse to the stabler

Travellers were forbidden by law to lodge with their friends. They had to stay in the hostelries except in special circumstances. Burgesses who gave lodging to their friends without permission were liable to a fine of forty shillings.

The inns had to provide stabling accommodation free, but the traveller paid for the corn and hay supplied. This was the reason why the inn-keepers of Edinburgh were often called stablers, a title which was still sometimes used in the nineteenth century.

There were also strict regulations about what people wore in the fifteenth century. Silk and fur were forbidden except for lords and knights. In 1457 parliament instructed the burgesses to make sure that their wives and daughters were dressed according to their station in life. They were not allowed elaborate or embroidered gowns or large head-dresses. Labourers and husbandmen had to wear grey and white on working days, but on holy days they were allowed light blue, green and red clothes.

THIS SCULPTURED STONE shows the simple bed and furniture of a merchant's house

Around 1500 the main street of Edinburgh was crowded by day with stallholders selling their wares. There were no shops. Some traders set up booths around St Giles'. Later on, when these became more permanent and could be locked, they were called *luckenbooths* or locking booths.

Fisherwomen shouted their wares side by side with fleshers and cloth-sellers. Beggars sought alms and minstrels performed their few tunes for gain. The street became so congested that in 1477 the town council specified the areas where various goods could be sold.

There are few records of entertainment up to the fifteenth century. Tournaments were held under the Castle rock. One is recorded in 1398 when Queen Annabella, wife of Robert III, saw twelve knights take part. One of them was her eldest son, Prince David.

TOURNAMENTS WERE HELD at the foot of the Castle rock

James IV often summoned the members of his court for jousting and presented awards of golden-tipped spears himself. The fame of these tournaments made Edinburgh an international city even in those days, and many foreign knights were encouraged to come for the sport.

During the thirteenth and fourteenth centuries Holyrood abbey and monastery were being completed, and the great new church was taking the place of the earlier, smaller church. Of this new church only the remains of the nave survive today.

During the second half of the fifteenth century the great abbot, Crawford, preserved the church by introducing the flying buttresses which today still bear his shield. His successor put on the lead roof which was stolen by the English troops under Hertford in the middle of the next century when the abbey was burned with the town.

St Giles' was the parish church of the burgh. Round it, where Parliament Square is now, were the houses of the clergy and the graveyard. St Giles' did not reach its present size until about 1558. The crown tower was put up in the fifteenth century.

ORGANS WERE USED IN CHURCHES as shown in this altar piece panel

TRINITY COLLEGE CHURCH was founded in 1460 by Queen Mary of Gueldres, wife of James II

Greyfriars from Holland built a convent in 1447 in the area next to the present Greyfriars Church. The Blackfriars or Dominicans settled in the Cowgate as early as 1230 on royal ground given by Alexander II.

Important visitors in medieval times often lived in the guest-houses of the convents. Kings and queens, ambassadors, papal delegates, princes and nobles were housed there when there was no palace to receive them and the accommodation at the Castle was too small.

THE RUINS OF ST ANTHONY'S CHAPEL

In the Canongate, the Knights of St John of Jerusalem maintained a preceptory from the early 1300s for a hundred years or so. Not far away was the hospital of St Mary, founded by the magistrates in 1438.

On a rocky hillside above St Margaret's Loch are the remains of St Anthony's chapel and hermitage. Little is known about it, but it was probably connected with a hospital for people suffering from erysipelas (which was then called St Anthony's fire). James I had certainly founded such a hospital in Leith about 1430.

There were other old foundations in the little villages and hamlets round the Edinburgh of this time, which are now within the boundaries of the modern city.

The old parish church at Restalrig dates back to the twelfth century and is traditionally the burying-place of St Triduana. In the fifteenth century sufferers from eye-diseases made pilgrimages to her well.

The church at Corstorphine was being built and tradition says that a lamp was lit high up on its east gable to guide travellers through the marsh.

ST TRIDUANA'S CHAPEL AND WELL to which people came to cure eye diseases. A statue of the saint is on top of the building

22

The original Duddingston church was erected in the twelfth century. Biblical pictures carved on its ancient doorway can still be seen.

In the fifteenth century, tower houses were built by the powerful nobles or families of the neighbourhood. Today their ruins are inside the city. Craigmillar Castle was associated with Queen Mary. For three hundred years it belonged to the family of Preston, several of whom became provosts of Edinburgh.

CORSTORPHINE CHURCH

The second Preston gave St Giles' Church an armbone of St Giles as a sacred relic. In recognition of the gift the Preston aisle of the church was built. It still exists today and now contains the royal pew.

Remains of other tower houses of this period exist at Liberton and Cramond, at Craiglockhart and Merchiston. The last was, in the next century, the home of John Napier, the inventor of logarithms.

MERCHISTON CASTLE is now part of a modern technical college named after Napier, the mathematician

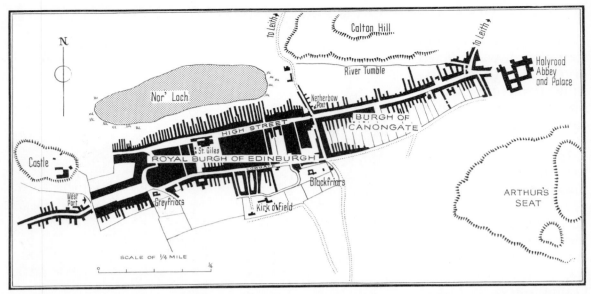

EDINBURGH IN THE SIXTEENTH CENTURY was becoming crowded. Everyone wished to live inside the walls

4. EDINBURGH TO THE UNION OF THE CROWNS

THE GOLDEN AGE OF JAMES IV

The sixteenth century in Edinburgh and in Scotland generally was a strange mixture. It opened with a period of great rejoicing which soon changed to despair, defeat, civil war and religious strife. It ended with a period of prosperity which lasted till the departure of the king to London in 1603.

The marriage of the Thistle and the Rose took place in 1503 in the abbey church of Holyrood. The people hoped that this union of the thistle, King James IV, with the rose, Princess Margaret Tudor, daughter of Henry VII, would bring to an end the long struggle with England.

For his bride the king had had the palace in the Castle repaired. The great hall, commonly called the banqueting hall of the Castle, was built during this period and the monogram and emblems of the king are carved on its walls.

MARGARET TUDOR ARRIVES IN PROCESSION for the marriage of the Thistle and the Rose

24

The Scottish poet, William Dunbar, wrote a poem to celebrate these events. The marriage was indeed important for from it came the Union of the Crowns of England and Scotland a century later.

The king also began building a palace beside the abbey. Before this there was no special royal residence at the abbey although the king and many important persons had been given lodging there. The tower he built still remains and contains the most historic apartments of the palace. Remains of his gateway still exist.

The reign of James IV has been called the golden age of Scottish medieval history. The king was the patron of the arts and education. He gave a charter to the Royal College of Surgeons of Edinburgh. He ordered all barons and labourers to see that their eldest sons stayed at school and college long enough to understand the laws. The Pope presented him with the sword of state which is still treasured in the Scottish regalia in the Castle.

THE FIRST PRINTING PRESS IN SCOTLAND was set up by Chapman and Myllar. It was similar to that used by Caxton in England

In 1507 the art of printing came to Scotland. The king granted the exclusive right to set up a printing press in Edinburgh to Walter Chapman, an Edinburgh merchant, and to Andrew Myllar, a bookseller. They did so in the Cowgate near where it meets the modern Blackfriars Street.

James was the father of the Scottish navy. His fleet of about thirty ships was led by the *Great Michael* built at the king's New-haven, adjoining Leith, a fishing harbour today.

The peace and prosperity of Edinburgh and its port of Leith were not to last. Henry VII died and his successor, Henry VIII, was soon in disagreement with the French who had been Scottish allies for a long time.

THE GREAT MICHAEL was the flagship of James IV's navy

King James IV was persuaded to invade England to assist the French. Part of his great army gathered on the Burgh Muir of Edinburgh. Disaster followed at Flodden Field in 1513. The king and many of the nobles were slain: magistrates and townsmen died with them. Edinburgh was grief-stricken.

Everyone in the burgh who could bear arms was summoned to be ready for its defence: the women were sent to church to pray for relief. A standing watch of twenty-four men was created, the original town guard.

A new wall, known as the Flodden Wall, was built round the town to resist an expected invasion. It included the new buildings of the Cowgate and the Grassmarket. Some remains still exist which show it was built in a hurry. Fortunately the burgh was not invaded for some years.

NAUTICAL INSTRUMENTS OF THE SIXTEENTH CENTURY are seen on this stone at Newhaven

IN THE TIME OF MARY QUEEN OF SCOTS

The new king, James V, was only an infant. There were many disturbances in Edinburgh as rival groups of noblemen struggled for power.

When he grew up, the king continued building the palace at Holyrood which his father had begun.

James V established in Edinburgh a court of fifteen new judges called the Court of Session, to deal with the complaints of the people. He arranged that the judges should be paid sufficiently highly for their work so that they would not need to take bribes. The Court of Session still meets today in the Parliament Hall buildings behind St Giles'.

THE WINDOW IN PARLIAMENT HOUSE which shows King James V creating the Court of Session

During the reign of James V the first protests in Scotland were made about the established religion of the Roman church. Sir David Lindsay, who had been the king's page and his constant companion, wrote many satirical works, the most famous being *The Satire of the Three Estates* which criticised the church and exposed corruption.

Some, however, who opposed the church were accused of heresy and condemned to be burned at the Castlehill of Edinburgh. This was the beginning of the troubled times which were to fall upon Edinburgh in the next reign.

THE PALACE OF MARY OF GUISE, CASTLEHILL

CARDINAL BEATON'S PALACE IN COWGATE

When James V died in 1542 he was succeeded by another infant, Mary, who was only a few days old. The struggle for power was renewed and Edinburgh suffered in consequence.

The Protestant party favoured an alliance with Henry VIII of England and promised that when Mary was old enough she would marry Prince Edward, the son of the English king.

The Roman church party, headed by Cardinal Beaton and the queen's mother, Mary of Guise, favoured alliance with France and managed to persuade the Scottish parliament to break the agreement with England.

King Henry immediately sent English forces to Scotland under the Earl of Hertford. They occupied Newhaven and Leith. Hertford demanded and was refused the care of the young queen. He attacked the Castle without success and then proceeded to burn the town.

As a result of this fire, which he continued for three days, only parts of the Castle, St Giles' and Holyrood remain today of the early city. Hertford returned three years later in 1547 and continued his destruction by burning Leith, making further devastation in Edinburgh and tearing the lead roof off the abbey of Holyrood.

THE TRIAL OF WITCHES

THE STATUE OF JOHN KNOX at New College

The young queen was taken to France at the age of six. Edinburgh was seldom free from disputes between rival noble families and their followers. The Reformation struggles were also increasing. Heretics were being burned on the Castlehill or at Greenside where James II had granted the burgh a place for tournament and sport.

John Knox returned to Edinburgh and began preaching against the Roman church. His popularity increased. The ranks of the Protestants grew in number and were difficult to control. They made an attack on St Giles'. The statue of the saint was stolen and thrown into the Nor' Loch, where offenders were often ducked, and then burned. Another statue carried in the annual procession of the saint received similar treatment. Damage was also done to altars and images in other churches of the town.

To rid the city and country of French troops the Protestants, or Congregation as they called themselves, appealed to Queen Elizabeth of England to help them. By the Treaty of Edinburgh of 1560 the French left and the Scottish parliament was free to declare Scotland a Protestant country.

MARY QUEEN OF SCOTS RETURNS FROM FRANCE. She is met at Leith

One year later Queen Mary returned from France, a young widow. She landed at Leith and went to Holyroodhouse. She only remained in Edinburgh for about six years but her activities had a lasting influence on the city.

She married her cousin, Lord Darnley, who was proclaimed king at the Mercat or Market Cross, in 1565. John Knox objected. He visited Mary at Holyrood and preached against her in St Giles'.

Mary's secretary, David Rizzio, was murdered in Holyroodhouse in her presence. Darnley was suspected. Mary retired to the Castle. In the small bedroom high up in the palace block she gave birth to her son James. He was to bring peace to the country and to become the first king of the united Britain which was to expand into the empire and the commonwealth as the centuries passed. Perhaps we can say that the British Commonwealth of Nations was born in this tiny room.

THE ROYAL ARMS in the small room in Edinburgh Castle where James VI was born. Notice the prayer beneath

INITIALS OF MARY AND HENRY, LORD DARNLEY, at the Palace in the Castle

MEN AND WOMEN OF THE SIXTEENTH CENTURY

Darnley caught smallpox and was kept in a house at Kirk o' Field, one of the friars' establishments, where the university now stands. Mary visited him and even slept in the house. One night, after she had left to attend an entertainment at Holyrood there was a loud explosion. The building was destroyed and Darnley dead.

Four months later, 16th June 1567, Mary left Holyrood for the last time, a prisoner of her lords. She had to give up her throne to her infant son.

In her short period Mary had made changes in Edinburgh. The tolbooth which had existed from the fourteenth century had become too small. Mary urged a new building for the use of the Court of Session and the town council.

In return for a loan of money, the magistrates obtained an important privilege. By the charter of 1329 they controlled the harbour of Leith. By the new gift they obtained control of the lands around the harbour. They had longed for this ground for many years so that they could develop the port.

Mary spent some time at Craigmillar Castle, now in the suburbs, and her French followers gave names to places nearby. At Little France the remains of a tree are shown which was planted by the queen.

THE OLD TOLBOOTH OF LEITH was an important building in the sixteenth and seventeenth centuries

The Castle continued to hold out for the cause of Mary under Sir William Kirkaldy of Grange. The old tower built by David II was strong enough to resist siege for three years.

English troops were again brought to the city. They poisoned the well at the Well-House Tower in Princes Street Gardens, and some lucky attacks by cannon-balls caused part of the tower to fall into the forewell. The other two wells were unusable as they were under fire. The Castle had to sur-render because of lack of water. Kirkaldy and others were hanged at the Mercat Cross and their heads were hung on the Castle walls.

FIRING THE ONE O'CLOCK GUN. The time gun has been fired from the Castle since 1861. It is in the Half-Moon Battery of the Castle which conceals the remains of David's Tower

It was not long before the Castle was restored by the construction of the prominent feature known as the Half-Moon Battery. It was built on the top of the remains of David's tower, which was forgotten, and only rediscovered in 1912. From this battery a gun is now fired daily at one o'clock.

LIFE IN THE SIXTEENTH CENTURY

At the beginning of the sixteenth century the houses of the burgh were still almost completely built of wood or wood and clay. Drawings show that perhaps none were more than two storeys high, sometimes with attics; most had thatched roofs, although some had tiles. Their gables mostly fronted the street and their gardens were behind. These houses burned easily in the Hertford invasions.

31

SIXTEENTH-CENTURY STREET SCENE. The houses have forestairs. Note the water-carrier

The houses were small inside. The main room of the house was a hall on the first floor. It served as the living-room. Adjoining it was a chamber (bedroom). Under the hall at street level were the cellars which served as stables, shops or store-houses. Attics were sometimes used as work rooms.

There was little furniture. At this time there was usually only one arm-chair for the head of the household and benches or stools for the others. Most of the possessions were kept in chests or kists instead of in cupboards or wardrobes as today. Many houses had forestairs to the first floor jutting out on to the roadway. Others had overhanging galleries supported on wooden posts.

JEWEL BOX OF MARY OF GUISE

In the latter half of the century, especially after the fire, the homes of the wealthy were built of stone. A large number of important people came to Edinburgh to be near the royal court and the new law courts. Many of them built new houses, but it was not until the next century that the houses became bigger and better furnished.

Merchants were also able to build better houses and some, considerably altered by time, survive. John Knox's house must have been begun just after the fire. Mowbray House next to it was probably of about the same date.

JOHN KNOX'S HOUSE. After the great burning of 1544 houses of wealthy merchants were built of stone as were John Knox's house and Mowbray House

In the burgh of the Canongate, Huntly House, now one of the city's museums, belongs to this period. Opposite is the Canongate Tolbooth, built in 1591, which housed the council chamber, courthouse and prison of the burgh of Canongate until the nineteenth century.

In Leith there is Lamb's House, much altered, where Mary Queen of Scots rested after she landed from France in 1561.

Bailie Macmorran's House is in Riddle's Court. The bailie was the unfortunate victim of the pupils of the Royal High School of Edinburgh. In 1595 the schoolboys were refused a holiday by the town council who were the governors of the school. They arrived early at school, and locked themselves in with plenty of provisions and firearms. When the master could not gain admittance the bailie was summoned.

HUNTLY HOUSE has been called the Speaking House because of the tablets on the walls which give good advice

When he ordered the door to be forced by the guard he was shot. This event troubled the city and the king. The king had only recently granted the title Royal to the old grammar school of Edinburgh, whose beginnings are unknown but go back to the foundation of the monastery of Holyrood itself.

THE HIGH SCHOOL BUILT IN 1578

Fights between noble families and their followers were not uncommon during the century. The streets and closes often rang with pistol shots. Perhaps the most famous occasion was the incident in 1520 called " Cleanse the Causeway ", when the parties of the Earl of Arran and the Earl of Angus met in the High Street. Arran, who was regent at that time, was driven out of the gates, narrowly escaping with his life.

THE TOLBOOTH WAS THE PLACE OF GOVERNMENT of the city and the prison. Its shape is marked on the street beside St Giles'. It was the *Heart of Midlothian* of Sir Walter Scott

FLESHMARKET CLOSE

The burgh was dirty. There was no proper sanitation and disease frequently spread quickly through the closes. The magistrates often reminded the inhabitants to keep the closes clean by removing their middens and filth. The medieval city must have been an unpleasant place in the heat of summer.

To try to make the burgh more pleasant for visitors and themselves the authorities had regulated the places where goods might be sold. The markets came to have fixed areas. Some of the names survive today, like Grassmarket, Fleshmarket Close, Fishmarket Close.

The rich and poor lived side by side in the old closes, even up the same stairs.

MERCHANTS AND CRAFTSMEN

The wealth of the merchants came from their overseas trade and their monopoly of the retail trade of the burgh. They brought fine dress materials from France, Flanders and Italy. They imported fruit, spices, vegetables and salt. The wine trade increased in value many times during the century.

THE WINE TRADE PROSPERED AT LEITH. The wine cellars at Leith are still in use today

The merchants had to risk much, especially piracy and attacks by English seamen. Many complained to the town council about their losses. Still, they were wealthy men. They built finer homes. They were able to lend money to the king on occasion. Some contributed to charity. Others, like Walter Chapman, the first printer, gave to the church. He built a chapel in St Giles'.

It was common for royalty to visit the houses of prominent citizens and Queen Mary even found refuge in one.

MERCHANTS' HOMES BECAME RICHER. Ceilings were often carved or plastered or painted. Chairs became more common

The merchants and craftsmen often disagreed. Only merchants could be magistrates. A craftsman could serve on the town council but he could not become a magistrate unless he gave up his craft.

This was hard on the craftsmen. In the sixteenth century the council consisted of the provost, four bailies, dean of guild, treasurer, ten merchants and eight craftsmen.

Besides having privileges, the merchants and craftsmen had responsibilities. They had the duty of guarding the royal burgh. They had to be prepared for duty in the royal army if required. They had to provide for the poor of their guild or craft. They had to pay taxes both to the town and to the crown.

According to the burgh records, when an English invasion was threatened in 1558 the merchants could offer 736 men and the crafts 717. Of the latter some were freemen and some servants. The numbers for the different crafts give some idea of the principal employment at the time. 178 tailors volunteered, 151 hammermen, 20 goldsmiths, 100 bakers, 49 cordiners (shoemakers), 53 bonnetmakers, 63 skinners and 9 furriers.

MAGDALEN CHAPEL, built *c.* 1541, was used by the hammermen. It contains the only important pre-Reformation stained glass in Scotland

Before the Reformation there was little education except in the grammar schools of Edinburgh, Canongate and Leith. After it, people began to care more about education. By 1590 the town council had established at least six ordinary schools to teach reading and writing.

THE HALL OF THE TAILORS

Seven years earlier the town had opened the University or Tounis College on the lands of Kirk o' Field, acquired from the queen in 1563. It was different from the other three universities in Scotland which had been founded by the church. Edinburgh University was a civic foundation.

Some of the sports and games popular at the beginning of the sixteenth century were banned by the end of it. The Reformation church played its part in making the changes. The celebration of May games, Queen of the May, Robin Hood and Little John vanished from the calendar.

DANCING ROUND THE MAYPOLE, AND OTHER GAMES, were banned by the Reformation Church

Golf was played on open ground and later on the links at Leith and Bruntsfield. Archery was by this time an amusement, although in the previous century it had been part of military training.

A game called catchpole, similar to tennis, was played on special courts in various parts of the town. Bowls, quoits and football were well known.

Pigeon shooting took place on the North Loch and other sheets of water. Children mostly played ball, and young children had rattles and dolls. Some of these were imported from other countries.

PIGEON SHOOTING at the North Loch

Pageants, plays and processions ceased after the Reformation. The early plays were mostly of the miracle or morality type. In 1508 the goldsmiths had a pageant of the passion. *The Satire of the Three Estates* was performed before the Queen Regent in 1554. The riding of the marches of the town took place on All Hallows' Even, the occasion of a great annual fair.

People spent much time drinking in taverns and singing songs and ballads. The rich had frequent banquets, often associated with royal occasions. The processions of distinguished visitors to the Castle or Palace up the West Bow and down the High Street were enjoyed by all. There was gaiety as well as tragedy in the sixteenth century.

THE MAIDEN WAS A SCOTTISH FORE-RUNNER OF THE GUILLOTINE. It was said to have been introduced by the Earl of Morton who was condemned to die by it in 1580

PUNISHMENTS HAD TO BE ENDURED IN THE STREETS. Passers-by jeered or stood and stared

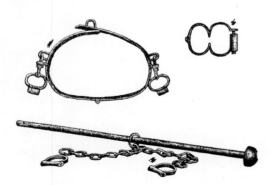

THE GIRDLE, FETTERLOCK AND IRON GUARD were commonly used for punishment

Punishment even for minor offences was often severe. A butcher who concealed a person suffering from the plague was branded publicly on both cheeks and banished from the town. A perjurer of 1561 was punished by having his tongue pierced. A woman was drowned for common theft. Ears were often cut off and persons had to endure whipping, the pillory and similar tortures.

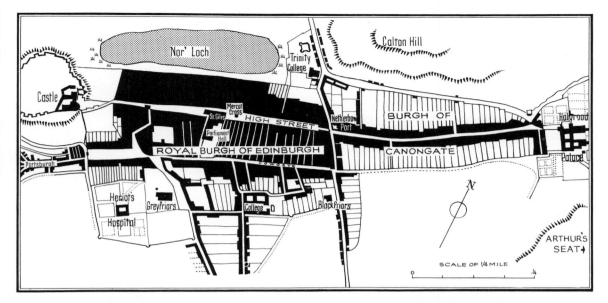

EDINBURGH IN THE SEVENTEENTH CENTURY. Little open ground still remained inside the walls

5. EDINBURGH TO THE UNION OF THE PARLIAMENTS

AFTER THE UNION OF THE CROWNS

The century from the Union of the Crowns in 1603 to the Union of the Parliaments in 1707 is as full of changing events as the previous one. Many of these events concern the country as a whole rather than Edinburgh in particular.

With the departure of the king in 1603 the older generation could look forward to the end of strife and to peaceful relations with the old enemy, England. The king promised that he would return every three years but it was fourteen before he did so. The removal of the court to London took away some of the prosperity of the town and reduced the number of social activities.

Parliament and the highest law courts of Scotland still met in Edinburgh.

THE ROYAL PROCESSION LEAVES HOLYROOD FOR LONDON. The King was not to return for fourteen years

39

Some merchants closely connected with the court, such as the goldsmith, George Heriot, the Jingling Geordie of Sir Walter Scott, also went south. Other people went in the hope of obtaining office in the new realm of Great Britain.

James tried to control Edinburgh from London, and he sent frequent requests and orders to the magistrates. In 1609 he ordered that the magistrates should wear robes like those of the aldermen of London and he gave authority for a sword to be carried in front of the provost on public occasions.

THE VAULTED GATEWAY OF HOLYROOD was built in 1502 and taken down in 1753. The south wall can still be seen

For his reception in 1617 the king had additions and alterations made to the palace in the Castle, including the building which contains the crown room. The king intended to show his English lords that Scotland and Edinburgh were no less civilised than London.

He also restored the room in which he was born and had his mother's and his own initials painted on the panelling of the ceiling. On the walls he put the date of his birth, 19th June 1566, and the royal arms.

ST GILES' was a cathedral for only a short time. In the seventeenth century it was shut in by high buildings and the broad High Street was narrowed

Charles I was crowned in the abbey of Holyrood. Like the other Stuart kings he favoured the episcopalian system of church government. He created a separate diocese of Edinburgh, with St Giles' as its cathedral. The name " cathedral " has wrongly been attached to St Giles' ever since. Its real name is the High Kirk of Edinburgh.

The presbyterians objected strongly to the reading of the episcopalian service book. The incident involving the cabbage-seller at the Tron, Jenny Geddes, took place in 1637. She is said to have flung her folding stool at the clergyman when he began to read. In these days there were no seats in churches and worshippers often provided their own stools.

SIGNING THE COVENANT AT GREYFRIARS

A SEVENTEENTH-CENTURY STOOL. Jenny Geddes threw such a stool in St Giles'

The feeling against episcopacy increased. When a royal proclamation to continue the use of the service book was made at the Mercat Cross in 1638 a protest was read by some opposing noblemen. The outcome was the drawing up of the National Covenant which was signed in and around Greyfriars Church.

This church had been opened in 1620 in the grounds of the old convent of the friars. Greyfriars was the first new church in Edinburgh after the Reformation. The next was the Tron Church, built to house a congregation which lost its place of worship when partitions were removed from St Giles' to make the cathedral. St Giles' was at one time divided into four churches.

CROMWELL IN EDINBURGH

Oliver Cromwell was the next prominent visitor to Edinburgh. He lodged at Moray House in 1648 and was entertained at the Castle. When the king was executed in the following year there was almost a separation of the two kingdoms. Charles II was proclaimed king at the Mercat Cross. Cromwell's forces marched north, fought the battle of Dunbar and proclaimed martial law in Edinburgh.

Cromwell was strict not only with the citizens but also with his own men. Men who stole from houses were scourged through the town and others were made to take their punishment at the Cross.

41

THE GATEWAY OF MORAY HOUSE

The occupation of Edinburgh by the English worried the town council. A number of fires occurred in buildings occupied by Cromwell's troops and furnishings of others were destroyed. Among the buildings affected was the palace of Holyroodhouse which was being used as a barracks.

English settlers followed the Cromwellian troops and came to live at Leith. They began to develop their own trading centre.

Leith was considered by Cromwell an important place for the defence of the country. The Edinburgh magistrates were alarmed as they owned the port and controlled the trade. They were anxious to preserve their rights. After much discussion Edinburgh built a citadel at Leith and kept her rights. The citadel disappeared long ago to make way for houses.

On the whole the burgh had peace during the protectorate and the magistrates were able to thank General Monk, the commander-in-chief, when he departed in 1659.

They were then secretly planning for the restoration of Charles II which they celebrated the next year with great enthusiasm. We are told that, on the day of the celebration, claret flowed from the spouts of the cross, tables were loaded, and an effigy of Cromwell was burned in a fireworks display at the Castle.

ENTRANCE TO THE CITADEL OF LEITH

THE RESTORATION AND EXPANSION

The rejoicing of Edinburgh soon turned to sadness in the religious strife that followed. The king again imposed the episcopalian form of church government on a people who stood for the principles of the Covenant.

Most of the fighting took place out of the capital but the prisoners were brought to Edinburgh. Many hundreds were shut up in a part of Greyfriars churchyard, still called the Covenanters' prison. They had to live in the open air with little food and no shelter from the weather. Many were tortured and executed in the Grassmarket where a memorial today reminds the passer-by of these grim, old days.

Charles II reconstructed the Palace of Holyroodhouse. Sir William Bruce was the architect, and the king's master mason, Robert Mylne, carried out the work. The palace was built as we see it today with a new tower to the east to match the old James IV tower at the west.

A Dutch artist, de Witt, was engaged to paint the kings of Scotland for the picture gallery. The ornamental plasterwork was by Englishmen: fireplaces came from Italy, glass from France and marble and tiles from Holland. The new palace blended with the old.

THE STATUE OF CHARLES II IN PARLIAMENT SQUARE is the oldest statue in Edinburgh. Notice the King has no stirrups

FORECOURT OF THE PALACE OF HOLYROODHOUSE as restored by Charles II

In 1667 the king gave the chief magistrate of Edinburgh the title of Lord Provost which each of his successors has borne. The records, however, show that the term had been used from time to time since 1553.

By the time of the Restoration the royal burgh was quite changed. It had extended beyond the old Flodden wall. In 1617 it bought the lands of High Riggs near Tollcross. In 1639 it bought the Canongate, Pleasance and North Leith, which included the Calton Hill. Portsburgh was purchased later.

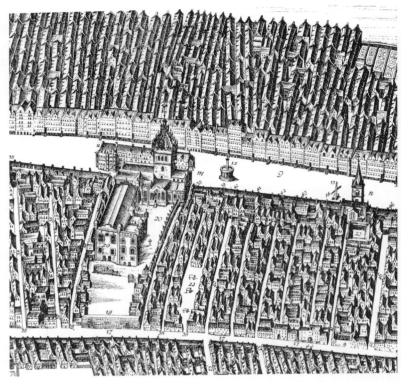

THIS MAP OF 1647 shows the high buildings of the town and how close together they were built. No. 20 is Parliament Hall; *m* is St Giles'; *u* is Heart of Midlothian; 12 is Mercat Cross; 13 is the Tron; 17 is Cowgate

These lands became part of the common good of Edinburgh, the property of the citizens. The town council chose the magistrates to administer them.

OLD HOUSES IN THE BURGH OF PORTS-BURGH. Note the forestairs and crow-stepped gables

Within the old town, houses now began to grow higher as there was no room to expand sideways within the walls. Buildings soared to four, five, six or more storeys and the gardens were used for extra building. Forestairs in front of the houses began to disappear and were later forbidden. Houses were now built of stone with slates or tiles for roofing. Many Scots who had been to England with the court adopted English or foreign styles.

Rooms were now better furnished. The dresser was introduced to display silver and china. The old chest or kist became a chest-of-drawers. Ceilings were plastered with ornamental designs or panelled in wood and painted. Carpets and rugs were laid on floors previously strewn with rushes. Walls were

A KITCHEN AND LIVING ROOM of the seventeenth century

plastered and often panelled in oak or in Memel pine. They were hung with tapestries. Pictures also became common.

Houses now had several rooms besides the hall and kitchen. Sanitation, however, continued to be unsatisfactory and it was not helped by the heads of condemned persons rotting on the gates and elsewhere. The magistrates tried to stop gardyloo, the act of throwing refuse from the windows, by fixing iron bars across the windows.

DISEASE AND CRIME

The plague which raged in the Middle Ages was often a dreaded scourge in Edinburgh. One memento often pointed out in the Canongate is the statue of a Moor on the front of a building. It may be only the sign of a long-forgotten tradesman or shopkeeper but the following story shows how serious the plague was.

THE STATUE OF THE MOOR IN THE CANONGATE

The Master of Grey was condemned to the gallows for leading a mob in an attack on the house of the provost. He escaped to Morocco to return in 1645 at the height of an outbreak of plague when only sixty men of the town were still fit to bear arms. Disguised as a Moor, he demanded a ransom from the burgh to refrain from attacking it. The provost's daughter, sick of the plague, was also demanded. The "Moor" promised to cure her or forgo the ransom money. She was taken to the Canongate where he nursed her, revealed his identity and married her.

ADVOCATES' CLOSE. In the seventeenth century there was a picture gallery in a house on an upper floor

The first scavenger in Edinburgh was appointed during the Cromwellian period but one was not enough. Parliament intervened in 1687 and the town council provided twenty carts, each with two horses, to remove the refuse each night. The citizens were taxed for this and the cleanliness of the streets and closes started to improve.

Water still had to be carried from the public wells or drawn from private wells in the gardens of the houses. Bathrooms were practically unknown. A traveller to Edinburgh of this time said that its buildings were probably the highest in the world, and that each stairway led to the rooms of twenty or thirty families. With so many people living in the area it was very difficult to get enough water and to improve sanitation.

A STREET SCENE in the seventeenth century, showing a water carrier, a public well and a sedan chair

The streets and closes were dark. When burgesses went from one place to another they generally employed link-boys to carry their lanterns. In Cromwell's time householders who lived on the first storey were compelled to put lighted lanterns at their windows from dusk till curfew. The owners of taverns had to display lights till ten o'clock.

During the day the streets were narrowed by the booths and stalls of the merchants and craftsmen. Beggars were numerous and a problem for the authorities. The town council tried to license those belonging to the town. In 1633 Paul's Work was opened as one of the first poorhouses in the burgh, and houses of correction were formed later.

CLOSES WERE DARK AND BADLY PAVED

There were many complaints about the bad workmanship of the craftsmen. Townspeople complained of bad shoes but the shoemakers blamed the tanners for producing bad leather.

PAUL'S WORK

SILK-HUNG BEDS were common in the homes of the wealthy merchants

The king did not trust Edinburgh craftsmen to repair a silk-hung bed at Holyrood. He brought to Edinburgh a group of Flemish cloth makers to raise the standards. Instructors in tanning and other trades followed. By the end of the century craftsmanship had improved.

OFFENDERS WERE OFTEN
DUCKED IN THE NOR'
LOCH

Punishments for crimes were severe by twentieth-century standards. Not infrequently ears were nailed to the tron. Tongues of false witnesses were bored with an iron. During the Protectorate, justice was no less severe.

For forging two half-crowns an English soldier was bound to the gallows naked, whipped, had his ears nailed to the post for an hour and then cut off. Bankrupts were put in the pillory at the cross wearing a yellow hat. Other offenders were treated to the mare and the jougs. The ducking-stool and similar water ordeals were often used. Hanging and burning were frequent.

THE STOCKS

The strangling and burning of witches was renowned in Edinburgh. The suspect often had thumbs and toes tied together and was flung into the Nor' Loch. If she floated she was guilty: if she sank she was presumably innocent: if she drowned she was definitely innocent, but the proof was too late. The poor witches who survived were burned on the Castlehill. It has been said that more witches were tortured on the Castlehill than in all the rest of Scotland. By 1670 people had become more understanding and tolerant, and the persecution of these unfortunate people died out.

BUILDINGS, POLITICS AND UNION

The finest surviving building of this period is probably George Heriot's School or Hospital. When George Heriot died he left a fortune to endow a hospital for orphan sons of Edinburgh's freemen. The building was dedicated in 1659 but not completed for about another half-century. It is now a boys' school but there are still foundationer scholars. Heriot's was the first of a long series of similar endowments in later years.

GEORGE HERIOT'S
SCHOOL

PARLIAMENT HOUSE was finished in 1639 and used
by the Scottish Parliament until 1707

Another building of the same period and architecture can scarcely be seen now. Charles I pressed the town council to provide more suitable accommodation for parliament than the tolbooth. A new parliament hall was built behind St Giles' but it is now hidden by the buildings of Parliament Square.

The great hall is used today by the legal profession in connection with the Court of Session.

The house of one merchant survives from 1631, Gladstone's Land in the Lawnmarket. It has been restored and shows the forestair, arcaded front, crowstep gables and rooms with painted ceilings. A noble dwelling of the same period is Moray House, which Cromwell made his headquarters. It still stands in the Canongate with its sharp-pointed, stone gate pillars, its beautiful plastered ceilings and its balcony overlooking the street.

GLADSTONE'S LAND HAS BEEN RESTORED

The Canongate Church was built to accommodate the people of the Canongate when they were expelled from the abbey church by James VII. James decided to restore the Order of the Thistle, the most ancient Scottish order of knighthood, and required the church as the chapel of the order. He also established a college of priests of the Roman church in the abbey. When, however, the news of the landing of the Prince of Orange was received in Edinburgh the mob destroyed the restored chapel and the students burned an effigy of the Pope.

King James fled the country but the Castle held out for his cause for some time. It was the scene of the secret meeting of the governor and Graham of Claverhouse (of the song *Bonnie Dundee*). The event is commemorated on the tablet at the postern gate high above Princes Street Gardens. The Castle finally had to surrender.

THE POSTERN GATE OF THE CASTLE

Towards the end of the century a great disaster befell Scotland, and Edinburgh in particular. Scottish trade had been declining. To improve the position an attempt was made to establish a trading centre in the Isthmus of Panama (or Darien).

DARIEN HOUSE STOOD IN BRISTO PLACE

50

This Darien scheme was opposed by the English parliament and traders. The Scots colonists who persisted and tried to make a success of it were defeated by the Spaniards and by lack of provisions.

The failure of the scheme was a great loss to Scots generally and especially to some Edinburgh merchants who sponsored it. Its failure, too, was a commercial reason for the last event of this era, the negotiations for a treaty of union with England.

The closes and wynds of old Edinburgh often heard bitter arguments about the proposed conditions of the treaty of union. There were several riots which expressed disapproval of the decisions of the Scottish parliament. Military guard had to be maintained in Parliament Close, at the gates and at the abbey church. The English agent was Daniel Defoe who lodged in Mowbray House.

The treaty was to have been signed in the small summerhouse, ornamented with lions, in the garden of Moray House. The feeling against the Union was so great that this treaty, probably the most important event in Scottish history, had to be signed in a cellar opposite the Tron Church.

THE SUMMER HOUSE IN THE
GARDEN OF MORAY HOUSE

SIGNING THE TREATY IN THE UNION CELLAR

The Scottish parliament met for the last time in the Parliament Hall in Edinburgh on 16th January 1707. Its departure to London completed the exodus of men of state begun at the Union of the Crowns a century earlier. The burgh lost its importance as the centre of national life, and commercial life suffered from a depression of trade.

TRADE AND TRAVEL

In the seventeenth century some institutions were founded which still influence the life of the city. In 1681 King Charles II granted a charter to the Merchant Company of Edinburgh. This enabled the merchants to strengthen their position against the craftsmen who already had powerful incorporations or societies. Before the end of the century the Merchant Company had over three hundred members, twenty of whom were women.

In 1694 the merchants received a sum of money from Mary Erskine, widow of James Hair, a druggist in the town, to provide for the maintenance of the daughters of burgesses. The money was used to found the Merchant Maiden Hospital which is now a girls' school named the Mary Erskine School after its founder. The arrangements for the control of the hospital were confirmed in the second last act of the Scottish parliament, in 1707.

CARTS WITH WHEELS WERE NOW USED INSTEAD OF SLEDS

PACKS WERE MOSTLY CAR-RIED ON HORSE-BACK

The Bank of Scotland began in 1695. Its first accountant was George Watson who, by his will, was the founder of another of the great educational charitable trusts belonging to the merchants of Edinburgh. Today both a boys' school and a girls' school bear his name.

The usual method of transport at the beginning of the seventeenth century was by horseback. Pack horses were used for the carriage of goods and sleds were common. There were few private coaches. The first public coach did not appear till 1610, when a foreigner from Pomerania obtained from the king the exclusive right to run a coach from Edinburgh to Leith at a charge of about twopence per person.

The town council granted similar licences at the restoration and later in the century. An advertisement in a paper of 1658 announced a stage coach between Edinburgh and London, once every three weeks.

In 1678 a stage coach journey to Glasgow was approved by the Privy Council to carry mails and passengers. Drawn by six horses, it left Edinburgh every Monday and returned on Saturday. The roads were bad and few people travelled.

STAGE COACHES about to depart on their journey

Industry was centred on the banks of the Water of Leith which supplied the power for the mills. Most mills ground grain but there were also waulk mills which cleaned and thickened cloth after it had been woven. The mills were mainly at the village of Dean, at Canonmills and at Bonnington.

Paper was made at the Dalry mills from rags which were often difficult to procure. A diarist tells us that eleven mills belonging to the burgh and five belonging to the Heriot Hospital were destroyed in a great storm, in 1659.

AN EARLY PAPER-MILL. The sheets are drained in the tray, pressed in the press, hung up to dry and bundled

53

CLOTHES WERE WASHED IN THIS WAY

By the time of the Union many of the old houses had been swept away. Tenement buildings of stone had become the usual form of dwelling. In the Canongate mansions were still built. Citizens, rich and poor, lived cheek by jowl.

Business was often transacted in the house, although many had stalls or booths in the street. Most merchants preferred to take up a position near the cross so that they could easily see people passing up and down the street with whom they might do business.

The richest had mansions in the Cowgate. It was easier to enter the Cowgate with a carriage than to get near the closes of the High Street. Edinburgh was the wealthy capital of a relatively poor country at the time of the Union of the Parliaments. Costly dress was often criticised. Ladies appeared in hooped dresses of rich brocade with coloured plaids. Men's jacket coats were long with full sleeves. They wore large hats, often with a feather, and they usually wore wigs.

Where coaches were used the lackeys often appeared in brilliant livery. Sedan chairs were introduced into Edinburgh in 1667.

Tea became the favourite drink of ladies at the end of the century. It took the place of the claret of earlier years. China cups were introduced instead of the tin, pewter or wooden mugs of old.

THE SEDAN CHAIR was convenient in the narrow lanes and closes

54

PART OF THE PROCESSION OF THE SCOTTISH PARLIAMENT

6. FROM THE UNION TO THE GOLDEN AGE

THE JACOBITE RISINGS

By the time of the death of Queen Anne and the accession of the first George, Edinburgh had become almost a provincial town, robbed of royal, state and parliamentary occasions. The supreme courts of justice and the General Assembly of the church still met in the capital, but Edinburgh's history became local rather than national.

Edinburgh was still largely a medieval walled town of two streets, High Street and Cowgate, joined by a number of wynds and closes. There were a number of small burghs round about, Canongate, Calton, Portsburgh, Broughton and Leith, and there were hamlets beside the mills.

The gates and walls were repaired to withstand an expected attack at the time of the 1715 Jacobite rebellion. The attack passed by the city, although unsuccessful attempts were made on the Castle and the citadel at Leith.

In 1736 the city experienced one of its most famous riots. When the mob became unruly at the hanging of a smuggler named Andrew Wilson, Captain Porteous of the town guard ordered his men to fire among the crowd. They killed six and wounded others. Porteous was tried for this and condemned to death. He was, however, reprieved by the queen who was acting as regent at the time.

The people did not like this. They set the door of the tolbooth on fire, pulled out Porteous and led him to the Grassmarket. He was hung on a dyer's pole with a rope taken from a shop in the West Bow. The ringleaders were never found.

THE PORTEOUS RIOT

55

Some people thought the ringleaders were men of importance, some dressed up in ordinary clothes and others in female garments. The matter was raised in parliament and the city was fined. The money was paid as a pension to Mrs Porteous.

The town walls were again hurriedly repaired in 1745 at the time of the second Jacobite rising. The city guard prepared for siege but the Highlanders entered the city at the Netherbow Port when the gate was opened to allow a coach to leave. Prince Charles Edward Stuart quickly followed and made his headquarters at the Palace of Holyroodhouse. His men were encamped towards Duddingston in the surrounding royal park.

At the Mercat Cross, with traditional ceremony, the heralds proclaimed his father King James VIII. The town council were forced to provide supplies for the army on promise of payment later. The wealthier citizens crowded to the palace. For a short time gaiety returned to Holyrood, but Charles soon departed with his army to his main objective, the city of London.

PRINCE CHARLES ENTERS EDINBURGH

When the Duke of Cumberland, pursuing Charles northward after the retreat from Derby, reached Edinburgh he, too, according to a newspaper of the time, gave a great ball at Holyrood.

After Culloden the scene was different.

A CHIMNEY SWEEP

At the cross of Edinburgh fourteen of the standards of the chiefs at Culloden were burned. Each was carried there by a chimney-sweep and that of Charles by a hangman. The chimney-sweeps were a highly honoured society recognised by their buckled knee-breeches, flat bonnets and, of course, ladders and ropes.

Holyrood gave refuge in 1795 to the Count of Artois, brother of Louis XVI, the murdered king of France, during the French revolution. He lived there through the courtesy of the British government until he returned to France as King Charles X, only to come back again an exile a few years later.

PEACE AND THE NEW TOWN

The failure of the '45 rebellion brought peace to Edinburgh, and, with the peace, the beginning of a new era of prosperity. There was now no longer need for a walled town. London was removing its gates and Edinburgh did likewise. The Netherbow Port was pulled down, but its clock was preserved and still records the time at the Dean College.

The population, about 50,000 in 1750, had doubled in the fifty years from 1700 and there was no room within the walls for expansion. The citizens were anxious to have more space and air about their houses, but the old rules compelled the burgesses to live inside the walls.

THE NETHERBOW PORT was demolished in 1764

Spring water had been brought to the burgh in 1676 from the springs named Fox, Hare, Swan and Lapwing at Comiston. The cistern was on the Castlehill and from there the water was piped to the city wells.

Trade was increasing and the leading citizens soon began to realise how inconvenient the old town was with its narrow entrances, streets and wynds. In 1753 the first of many Improvement Acts was passed. A large number of commissioners were appointed to advise on the erection of suitable public buildings and on proper access to the town from all directions.

The first improvement was the building of the Exchange for the merchants, which today is used as the City Chambers. The rubbish from the demolished buildings and from the foundations of the new buildings went to form the Castle esplanade. Curiously enough, the merchants were not keen to use the new Exchange. They preferred to continue their business in the open, where they could see everything that was happening and find their customers, especially their debtors.

THE ROYAL EXCHANGE BECAME THE CITY CHAMBERS

The king's master mason had planned a new housing scheme on the Castlehill at Mylne's Court around 1690, and James' Court was modernised a little later. Private builders grew busy to the south of the Cowgate, in the narrow area of land towards the Burgh or South Loch where today is the public park, the " Meadows ".

BROWN SQUARE, described in 1764 as a very elegant square of poets, writers and judges

Small squares were built and some private citizens moved to these from the congested old town. The Royal Scottish Museum now stands on the site of Argyle Square: Adam Square and Brown Square were at opposite ends of Chambers Street. Nicolson Square still exists. The largest and grandest was George Square which James Brown built on land which the town council had already refused to buy.

The Lord Provost, George Drummond, who was to be Lord Provost for six terms of office, was keen to build a bridge across the valley of the Nor' Loch, which had been partly drained in 1762. This would give better access to the lands to the north, the George Street area of today, where he hoped a new Edinburgh would arise. The new bridge would also give better access to the port of Leith, and thus improve trade and commerce.

Parliament approved this extension of the royalty of Edinburgh in 1767 and the town council lost no time in getting to work.

A competition for a plan of the new town was held. It was won by James Craig, a young twenty-seven-year-old architect. The plan was shown to the king, who approved it. It was a grid-iron plan with squares at each end. This was one of the very first pieces of deliberate town-planning in the country. Its wide streets and spacious squares are a valuable asset to Edinburgh today.

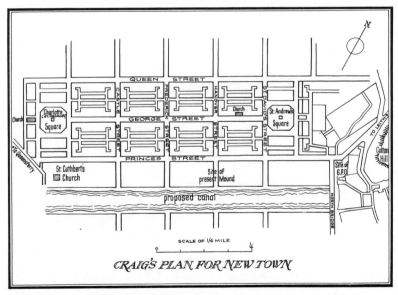

CRAIG'S PLAN FOR NEW TOWN

Even the street names were deliberately planned. The main street was called George Street after the king. On one side was Queen Street and on the other Princes Street called after his consort and the Prince of Wales. Between these were the narrower streets called Rose Street and Thistle Street after the emblems of England and Scotland. The patron saints were remembered in the great squares at the ends, St Andrew Square and St George's Square (now Charlotte Square). The whole was intersected by Hanover Street, after the name of the royal line.

The town council offered a prize of £20 to the first person to build a house in the new town. It was won by Mr James Young who built at Thistle Court, just off St Andrew Square. The first man to build in Princes Street was relieved of paying city rates.

Building continued during the next forty years. Princes Street was finished by 1805. The height of the buildings was limited to three storeys in the main streets and to two storeys in the side streets. Dormer windows were not allowed. There must have been a certain dull uniformity about the houses. As time passed, instead of designing individual houses the architects designed units of several houses. Bow windows were introduced in Castle Street.

Charlotte Square displayed the finest architectural design. It was the work of Robert Adam, the most eminent architect of his time. Each side of his square was a unit with classical façade and decoration. Unfortunately, Adam died before his work was finished. The north side is the finest and is protected today by law from any alteration. Architects and people from all over the world come to admire and examine it.

NORTH SIDE OF CHARLOTTE SQUARE, one of the finest street fronts in Europe

60

While this great new town was being built to the north the city obtained permission to open up a new street to the south. It began at the Tron Church, opposite the new North Bridge. It was also a bridge. There were twenty-two arches, but only one of them can be seen, where the roadway spans the Cowgate.

THE FIRST NORTH BRIDGE

This gave easier access to the new squares to the south and it made it easier to build a new college in 1789 on the Kirk o' Field site to replace the original houses which by then were ruinous. This building is what is now known as the Old College of the University.

The rubbish from the new town and other works was dumped in the middle of Princes Street at the Mound. This reduced the size of the Nor' Loch, which finally disappeared to become Princes Street Gardens. The Mound also gave another new entrance to the old town. The Burgh Loch was drained to become the Meadows and this gave easier access to the Burgh Muir and the south.

The old town was being neglected. Houses, previously occupied by the nobility, men of state and rich merchants, were now let to tradesmen, shopkeepers and working-class tenants.

THE MOUND grew up as a new link to the old town

Owners were no longer content with one or two rooms in the house. The hall and the chamber had given way to dining-room, drawing-room and several bedrooms, while the kitchen, cellars and attics had become the kitchen, scullery, laundry, stable, coachhouse and servants' rooms. Piped water had now come to the houses. Windows were larger. Roadways were wider and fresh air was able to circulate.

Many of Edinburgh's famous buildings date from this period. It was a time when the wealthy in the city were prepared to invest their money in buildings or to give lavishly for public buildings. The government built the General Register House for the preservation of the public records of Scotland. The architects were the Adam brothers.

ST GEORGE'S
CHURCH

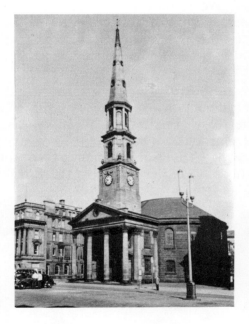

ST ANDREW'S
CHURCH

The two great churches of the new town, St Andrew's and St George's, now joined in union, were built in this period. The bells of St Andrew's were said to have given Nathaniel Gow the idea for the tune of the famous Scots song *Caller Herrin'*. St Andrew's Church was also the scene of the disruption of the Church of Scotland in 1843 when Dr Chalmers, whose monument is in George Street, led over four hundred ministers and elders out to form what became the Free Church of Scotland, independent of the patronage of the state.

By 1800 many other neighbourhood schemes were in progress or being discussed. The town expanded northwards from Queen Street and westwards towards the Water of Leith valley. Streets like Moray Place provided even more palatial homes for the wealthy. Classical architecture was predominant and stone, from Craigleith Quarry, not far away, was ideal for these new buildings.

ROYAL HIGH SCHOOL founded in the twelfth century was completed in 1829

The neighbourhood of the Calton Hill was designed on classical lines by William Playfair. Thomas Hamilton built the Royal High School whose central hall is a copy of the Temple of Theseus on the Acropolis of Athens.

Greek monuments were also the models for the Burns and Dugald Stewart monuments. The new observatory had classical porticos, and right at the top of the hill columns were erected in the style of the Parthenon, a memorial to the dead of the Napoleonic wars.

To gain access to the hill, a new road was made from what is now the General Post Office. This new road led to a new jail which replaced the old tolbooth, the Heart of Midlothian, adjacent to St Giles. The Calton Jail itself disappeared in the twentieth century to make room for St Andrew's House, the Whitehall of Scotland. Only the governor's house remains, a castellated structure clinging to the top of the cliff.

VIEW FROM CALTON HILL TO PRINCES STREET. The Calton Jail is in the centre

On the site of the General Post Office stood the Theatre Royal, in what was known as Shakespeare Square. It was built in 1768 and was the first licensed stage in Scotland. It became a centre for the new town. When Mrs Siddons performed,

THE THEATRE ROYAL was demolished to make way for the new G.P.O.

queues formed overnight for tickets. It is said that even the General Assembly of the Church regulated its proceedings to enable ministers to attend, a complete change of attitude from earlier times.

Although plays had been performed in Edinburgh before the Reformation, the Scottish Church disapproved of the stage. James VII had resident players at Holyrood. Occasionally strolling players came to the town and performed where they could find accommodation.

THE STATUE OF ALLAN RAMSAY

Allan Ramsay, whose statue is at the Mound beside the floral clock, tried to start a theatre in 1736 at Carrubber's Close, but it was closed by the magistrates. As plays could not be performed by themselves they were often staged free at the end of concerts in places like the hall of the Incorporation of the Tailors in the Cowgate.

A theatre did open in the Canongate at Playhouse Close in 1747. Despite many attempts to force it to close, it survived until the new theatre at Shakespeare Square was opened. Names associated with this old playhouse include David Garrick and John Home. Home was the author of the tragedy *Douglas*, which caused such resentment that the presbytery of Edinburgh censured the ministers who had seen it.

Allan Ramsay started the first lending library in Scotland in his shop opposite the Mercat Cross. It became a meeting-place for many of the Scottish wits of the time.

These library meetings often developed into convivial gatherings and many clubs were formed around men like Ramsay and others. Some of them had curious names like the Poker Club where new members were initiated with a poker as a mace, the Mirror Club which issued a magazine called the *Mirror*, the Wig Club which had as its symbol a supposedly ancient wig, the Crochallan Fencibles of which Robert Burns became a member, the Right and Wrong Club and so on.

ALLAN RAMSAY'S SHOP

None of the clubs has survived except the Speculative Society which was started in 1764 by some students of the University to give themselves practice in public speaking. It still meets today in the University by candlelight. It has had on its roll of members most of the great names of Scotland of the last two centuries.

MEDAL OF THE EDINBURGH REVOLUTION CLUB

The social life of society was strictly controlled in the eighteenth century. Edinburgh had several Assembly Rooms in succession. In each room or hall some lady presided and decreed the order and performance of the dance.

Ladies would arrive in their painted sedan chairs wearing their powdered wigs, hooped dresses, silk stockings and richly decorated petticoats. They would be accompanied by valets and link-boys to light the way. Gentlemen would be equally correct in their attire. They wore their swords at their sides, embroidered waistcoats, tight knee-breeches, three-cornered hats and dressed wigs. Ladies and gentlemen waited at opposite ends of the hall and could not meet without permission.

PORTOBELLO POTTERY. Clay from Portobello has been used since 1765

OLD ASSEMBLY ROOMS, WEST BOW. This narrow street was the principal entrance to the city for centuries

There were Assembly Rooms in the West Bow, at Assembly Close in the High Street, at Buccleuch Place for the residents of the George Square area, and in the new town where they are still the scene of the capital's finest social occasions.

Another form of entertainment took place in the oyster cellars where ladies and gentlemen sat round large tables enjoying oysters. They drank porter and punch. When conversation flagged, reels were danced until it was time to call the coaches. These gatherings were distinguished by their lack of formality compared with the regulation at the Assembly Rooms.

The Musical Society of Edinburgh, which originally met in one of the taverns, built St Cecilia's Hall in Niddry Street in 1762. Its concerts included the works of Corelli and Handel, Mozart and Beethoven. Many of these were first performances in Scotland.

OYSTER SELLERS AT LEITH. The oyster beds in the Firth of Forth were once very profitable

DANCING AT ST CECILIA'S HALL

The demand for tickets was so great that ladies were asked to attend without hoops in their dresses. In front was a space for parking sedan chairs, the forerunner of the modern car park.

THE MUSIC HALL

When the new town Assembly Rooms, and later the adjoining Music Hall, were built, St Cecilia's Hall was forgotten. The University of Edinburgh now owns it and has restored it as a musical centre.

Towards the end of the eighteenth century the old inns were changing into the more modern hotels. The inns were mostly grouped together at the gates of the town, in the Grassmarket–Candlemaker Row area and at the Pleasance–Netherbow area. Each inn provided stabling for horses. The best bedrooms were generally just above the stables.

Business improved with the introduction of the stage coach, and the proprietors of inns tried to persuade the coach owners to start from their premises. It was to such an inn that Dr Johnson came with Boswell. He lodged in the modern St Mary's Street at White-horse Inn or Boyd's Inn. (Most of the inns were known by the names of the owners.) Boyd's Inn was a terminus for a London coach which did the journey in four days in summer for a fare of £5 per seat. Coaches also went to Aberdeen, the Borders and Leith.

MEMORIAL TABLETS which may be seen at: **A** 32 York Place **B** 42 Lothian Street **C** the corner of Guthrie Street and Chambers Street **D** in Canongate Churchyard **E** 231 High Street

The George Inn at the old Bristo Port is featured in *Guy Mannering*, and the Whitehorse at the foot of the Canongate in *Waverley*. In the new town, hotels grew up. With the advent of the railways in the next century, the coach and carrier business of the inns declined.

The character of Edinburgh changed with the Golden Age. The city became a kind of literary metropolis and the home of publishing. Allan Ramsay's attempts to start a theatre have already been described. Smollett lived in the Canongate in 1776 and Oliver Goldsmith spent two years in Edinburgh studying medicine, although he was better known for his social gifts.

Adam Smith, the author of *The Wealth of Nations*, who advocated free trade and new ideas on economics, David Hume, the philosopher, historian and sceptic, Henry Mackenzie, author of *The Man of Feeling*, who recognised the greatness of the poet Burns, all lived in Edinburgh during the eighteenth century.

The poems of Robert Fergusson, over whose grave in Canongate Churchyard Burns erected a memorial, and the controversial translations of James Macpherson were discussed in the taverns.

Creech published the first Edinburgh edition of Burns and the works of Dugald Stewart the philosopher. Towards the end of the century Burns was the idol of Edinburgh society. Another great figure was Sir Walter Scott who, when he was a boy, met Burns in Professor Ferguson's house in Sciennes.

Sir Walter Scott increased the prestige of Edinburgh and Scotland by his romantic poems and novels. Born in Edinburgh, he was a pupil of the Royal High School. He arranged the royal visit of King George IV in 1822, the first royal visit for over a century.

ANCHOR CLOSE where *Encyclopaedia Britannica* was first printed in 1814. It was originated by Andrew Bell, an engraver

GEORGE IV ARRIVES IN EDINBURGH

By his influence, the crown room at the Castle was unsealed and the ancient honours of Scotland discovered. They have been on display ever since. Scott immortalised his native city, and created or revived a host of characters to people its streets and closes.

New buildings of the eighteenth century included a fine Royal Infirmary, a hall for the physicians and a royal dispensary. The surgeons were incorporated by a royal charter.

Edinburgh Chamber of Commerce began in 1786. The Blind Asylum opened in 1795.

THE LEITH RACES. Races were held at Leith from early in the seventeenth century until 1816 when the Edinburgh Race Meeting was transferred to Musselburgh where it is still held

Numerous societies began to study antiquarian, medical, legal and scientific subjects. The most important was the Royal Society of Edinburgh, begun in 1783, which is still the premier scientific society in Scotland.

The Edinburgh Society for the promotion of arts, science and manufactures held an industrial exhibition in 1756. This was one of the first exhibitions held in the country and may be compared with the modern trade fair.

The first School of Design was begun in Edinburgh in 1760, eight years before the Royal Academy in London. Edinburgh was a centre of activity in its Golden Age.

EDINBURGH AT THE END OF THE EIGHTEENTH CENTURY. This drawing was made by a Frenchman who saw Edinburgh as a city of skyscrapers

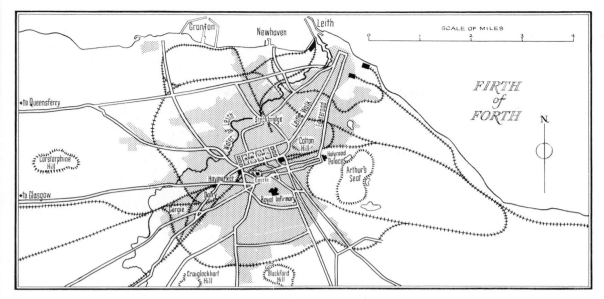

THE EXTENT OF EDINBURGH AT THE TIME OF THE INDUSTRIAL REVOLUTION

7. THE NINETEENTH CENTURY AND THE INDUSTRIAL AGE

THE BEGINNING OF THE INDUSTRIAL REVOLUTION

Near the harbour entrance of Leith the remains of a strong Martello tower still stand, a symbol of the troubled times at the beginning of the nineteenth century. After the French revolution the long war with France caused distress. The Edinburgh Volunteers were formed to defend the city and could regularly be seen drilling at Bruntsfield Links and at Leith.

The war cut off some supplies and the harvests were bad. In 1800 there was an oatmeal famine and meal mobs raided the stores of grain dealers on several occasions.

To relieve the poverty, the town council opened soup kitchens, but conditions did not really improve for many years. The working classes suffered badly, but work was found for them in making roads on the Calton Hill and in Holyrood Park and in laying out Bruntsfield Links.

In 1818 work began on the Union Canal, to connect Edinburgh with the Forth and Clyde Canal and Glasgow. Meetings to discuss railway projects were also common.

THE MARTELLO TOWER was once out at sea. The reclaimed land of the modern docks now reaches it

71

In 1826 a bill was passed for a railway between Edinburgh and Dalkeith with its terminus at St Leonard's. This was the first railway in Scotland. It is said to have obtained the nickname of the *Innocent Railway* because no passenger was injured on it. It was later extended to Leith and Fisherrow in 1833. Although it carried passengers its main purpose was to carry coal cheaply from the collieries at Newbattle.

THE INNOCENT RAILWAY runs through Holyrood Park between Samson's Ribs and the Wells o' Wearie. It enters a tunnel to reach its terminus at St Leonard's

Waverley Station was begun in 1836 when a tunnel was made under St Andrew Square to take a line to Leith and Newhaven. The Edinburgh to Glasgow railway opened in 1842 and Edinburgh was connected to London by the east coast in 1846. Two years later the Caledonian lines to Carlisle and the west coast began.

The building of the railways took away money which might have been used to develop the new town, many of whose streets were never finished. For example, it ended the scheme for a great new city stretching from the Calton to Leith.

The discovery of steam power also changed industry in Edinburgh. Mills were no longer dependent on the water power of the Water of Leith and other streams. Engineering works grew up at Sciennes and elsewhere. Printing, milling and other trades were all affected.

There was a great influx of labourers for these works, many of them Irish, and accommodation had to be found for them. The High Street dwellings were sub-divided and they deteriorated. New suburbs speedily grew up round the railways and canal, at Fountainbridge, Dalry, Gorgie, Stockbridge, Abbeyhill and St Leonard's. The face of Edinburgh was changed.

GORGIE SHOPPING CENTRE

TRANSPORT AND LIVING CONDITIONS

The steep, narrow street called the Upper Bow had been used for centuries as the ceremonial entry to the city. A new, broad approach road was now made to sweep round the Castle rock by Johnston Terrace. George IV Bridge was also built across the Cowgate valley. It has ten arches but today they are nearly all hidden by buildings. Lothian Road and Minto Street extended the access to the south.

THE DEAN BRIDGE

The Dean Bridge, designed by Telford, 110 feet high, crossed the deep gorge of the Water of Leith. It gave a new road to Queensferry and opened up the way for the development of Craigleith, Blackhall and Davidson's Mains. These new roads and bridges were all great engineering feats for their time.

Now that streets were wider and bridges spanned the deep valleys of the town, carriages became more common. By the middle of the century the sedan chair had almost disappeared.

In front of the doors of houses in the new streets, the pavement often projected far enough to allow the passengers of carriages to step right on to it. This was to save ladies' dresses being soiled in the gutters or on the actual street. The sedan chair was usually carried right into the lobby or hall of the house.

| EDINBURGH | LEITH | PORTSBURGH | CALTON | CANONGATE |

Badges displayed on windows in Edinburgh City Chambers

The carriages had curious names. The brougham was a one-horse vehicle called after Lord Brougham, an Edinburgh boy who became Lord Chancellor. The phaeton was four-wheeled, with either one or two horses. The noddy had two wheels, with its door at the back and the minibus was side-seated.

A FOUR-IN-HAND AND OTHER HORSE CARRIAGES IN PRINCES STREET

AN OLD HORSE BUS

Buses drawn by two horses now plied regularly to Leith. A new route crossed the city from Stockbridge to Newington. The drivers and conductors of the buses wore red coats and white hats, a reminder of coaching days. They blew a horn to warn of their approach.

The affairs of the town at this time were still controlled by a town council which did not represent the inhabitants. The citizens had no say in the election of the councillors. The council was responsible for light, water, streets, police, education, the poor, trade and the port of Leith.

In 1771, householders in the suburbs elected Police Commissioners to administer their districts when they did not come under the town council. They dealt with the lighting, policing and cleansing of their areas and could levy rates on their people for these services. This was the beginning of the system of rating we have today.

HIGH SCHOOL WYND, 1837

Political agitation, partly inspired by the French revolution, led to a desire for reform of national and local government. By the Burgh Reform Act of 1833, owners and occupiers of certain premises elected the town council. The city was divided into districts called wards.

LEITH ROADS 1824.   Note the early steam paddle boat

At the same time Leith was created a separate burgh.   For a long time the inhabitants had been protesting about their treatment by Edinburgh.   The docks and trade, which had been the privilege of the royal burgh from earliest times, had seven years before come under the control of a new body called the Leith Dock Commission.   Under the Commission they were extended and developed in the next hundred years.

The next development was in 1856 when the burgh was extended and the police commissioners and the town council were amalgamated.

The majority of the people still lived in unsatisfactory houses, especially in the old town.   Sanitation was inadequate.   The new inhabitants allowed property to deteriorate.   Closes, stairs and houses were dirty.   More air and fresher air was required in the wynds and alleys.   The keeping of pigs was forbidden.

Old property was demolished.   The luckenbooths disappeared and St Giles' could be seen again.   The old tolbooth was demolished in 1815.   Great fires in 1824 and 1825 were disastrous, but they helped to remove inferior property.

Despite all efforts, a serious cholera epidemic in 1832 caused six hundred deaths in Edinburgh in six months.

ALL HALLOWS' FAIR IN THE GRASSMARKET was stopped early in the nineteenth century

THE TRON CHURCH
was destroyed
by fire in 1824

A plentiful supply of water was required. The Edinburgh Water Company was formed in 1819, and by 1821 water was being brought from the Glencorse springs. Although water could then rise by gravitation to many houses there were still wells in the streets. More reservoirs were built in the Pentland Hills as the town increased in size. The water caddies who carried water in the previous century disappeared.

In earlier centuries, householders had to help to light the streets. Candles were mainly used up to the eighteenth century. The candle-makers whose old hall stands in Candlemaker Row were prosperous. Oil lamps were also used. Whale oil was common but there were complaints about the smell.

GLENCORSE
RESERVOIR

Lamps were lit and cared for by lamplighters called learies, one of whom was immortalised in a poem by Robert Louis Stevenson.

By 1818, some shops and streets were lit by gas made at the gas-works built off the Canongate. Soon houses also installed gas. Princes Street was lit by gas in 1822.

After Flodden, a town guard was formed to be a standing watch in the burgh. Under the original law every able citizen had to take his turn. This proved inadequate, and by 1690 a special military body replaced the old system. This town guard, which the poet Fergusson called " the black banditti ", lasted till 1817.

A LEARIE

THE TOWN GUARD HOUSE. At the side is the mare used for punishment

It had its headquarters in a low building obstructing the street near the tron. There, many punishments were carried out. The old guard was out of place by the nineteenth century, with its old-fashioned muskets, Lochaber axes and quaint military uniform.

In 1824, after the great fires which destroyed so much of the High Street and caused so many deaths, Edinburgh established a fire brigade. This was the first municipal fire brigade in the world. Previously citizens had to keep ladders available for fire-fighting. When fire insurance began, the companies kept their own engines and apparatus. They also fixed plates to the walls to distinguish properties insured by them.

The police commissioners prepared rules and set up fire stations. This did much to reduce the loss of property. The early engines were, of course, worked by man power. The first horse-drawn, steam fire-engine did not appear in Edinburgh till 1873, and it was forty years later that the first motor engine was bought. It was a grand sight to see the horse-drawn engines racing through the streets to a fire.

EDUCATION AND FAMOUS MEN

Some men who have left their mark on national, as well as local, history walked in the streets of Edinburgh at the beginning of the century.

Many of them visited the studios of Sir Henry Raeburn, a poor boy born at Stockbridge, who became a portrait painter. Neil Gow, the noted violin player and composer, sat for his portrait. Henry Mackenzie, Walter Scott, David Hume and James Boswell were among his literary subjects. Legal and parliamentary sitters were Lord Erskine and Lord Cockburn, Lord Jeffrey and Lord Melville, while there was a host of professors, ladies, merchants and others.

CRAIGCROOK CASTLE, home of Lord Jeffrey

Scott suffered from the financial collapse of his publishers, Ballantyne, but recovered to become the literary giant of the romantic movement. His monument, in Princes Street, perhaps the greatest to a man of letters, was inaugurated in 1846 by Lord Provost Adam Black.

THE SCOTT MONUMENT

LORD PROVOST ADAM BLACK, publisher

Francis Jeffrey and his friends Brougham, Sidney Smith and others founded the *Edinburgh Review* in 1802 in his flat at 18 Buccleuch Place, just off George Square. This journal became known throughout the kingdom for its criticism and opinion.

Lord Cockburn wrote memoirs which gave a personal picture of the life of his times. He wished to

THE WATT INSTITUTION AND THE SCHOOL OF ARTS

improve the amenity of the city, and the Cockburn Association was named after him. It watches over the interests of the citizens.

In 1821 the Edinburgh School of Arts was formed through the influence of Leonard Horner. Its purpose was to help workmen to learn the principles of science, mechanics, physics and chemistry, so that they could apply theory to practice and make themselves better tradesmen. Large numbers of mechanics attended classes each evening and when they discovered they could not understand elementary mathematics they formed classes for this also.

On the pattern of the Edinburgh School of Arts, Mechanics' Institutes were founded all over the British Isles. In time the School became the Watt Institution, in memory of the great discoverer of steam power. Later it was named the Heriot-Watt College, and gradually achieved university status.

Other bodies organised similar classes for adults at this time. Many were merely intended to teach reading and writing. One group, however, grew into the Edinburgh Philosophical Institution which included among its presidents and lecturers a number of prime ministers and leading authors of their time.

In connection with this movement for adult education, the Edinburgh Mechanics' Subscription Library was opened in 1825. The initial supply of books was given by the publishers Black and Constable for the use of all the working men of the city.

This library had the largest circulation in the United Kingdom by the middle of the century, and only closed in 1893 after the new free public library was opened.

Young men and women often founded Mutual Improvement Associations or literary and debating societies. Some of these published magazines which were circulated among the members.

Industry was expanding and the population was increasing. In 1750 there were about 50,000 people in Edinburgh: in 1850 there were 160,000.

School education was unsatisfactory for many children. There was supposed to be a school in each parish but not sufficient were provided. The system broke down despite the help from charity and private schools.

The University was famous for its medical discoveries. Great names such as the Munros, Gregory and Goodsir were outshone by Sir James Y. Simpson who in 1847 made the great discovery of the use of chloroform in surgery and midwifery. A little later Lord Lister saved many lives by his discoveries in the field of antiseptics. In other faculties men such as Blackie, Wilson (Christopher North), and Playfair were teachers of world-wide influence.

SIMPSON DISCOVERS THE EFFECTS OF CHLOROFORM

Alexander Graham Bell, inventor of the telephone, was an Edinburgh boy. So was James Clerk-Maxwell, the discoverer of the wireless ray.

NEW STREETS, HOUSES AND SCHOOLS

Several reports were written about the poverty of many of the inhabitants and the squalor in which they lived, but the public conscience was not aroused till, in 1861, a tenement in the High Street collapsed. Thirty-five people were killed. One young lad was saved by crying to the rescuers to " heave awa' " as he was not yet dead. The event is commemorated by a sculpture of the boy's head on the modern entrance way.

After public protests, the city appointed its first medical officer of health, who was the famous Sir Henry Duncan Littlejohn. Closes were now better paved and drained.

DOWIE'S TAVERN, LIBBERTON'S WYND 1854

LORD PROVOST CHAMBERS, publisher

Water and gas were installed in houses and the law insisted on the cleansing of stairways. The number of people in each apartment was controlled to avoid overcrowding.

In 1867 an Improvement Act was passed under Lord Provost Chambers, by which streets were driven through the most crowded areas. The old wooden fronts of tenements were removed and open spaces replaced ruinous buildings. Eleven new streets were made, including Chambers Street, called after the Lord Provost. New houses were erected, the beginnings of the great tenement schemes of late Victorian Edinburgh.

Travel became easier. There had been at least thirty-five tolls in what is now Edinburgh but by 1854 they had all been abolished. This made travel cheaper and we find two-horse buses on such journeys as Edinburgh to Leith.

THE HIGH STREET IN THE NINETEENTH CENTURY

The hansom cab was introduced for fast communication. Tramcars drawn by horses made their appearance in 1872. Trace-horses were added at the steeper slopes. The corporation took over the trams towards the end of the century. Shortly afterwards they introduced cable traction whereby the trams were pulled along by a cable under the street.

Meantime the port of Leith was expanding. In 1799, Edinburgh had consulted the great engineer, John Rennie, on how to provide berths for larger ships. Two docks, the East and West Old Docks, were constructed by 1817, but were abandoned when ships became larger. Three other docks were built on reclaimed land before 1900, and in 1904 the Imperial Dock was opened. Its entrance was seventy feet wide to take the large vessels used in overseas trade.

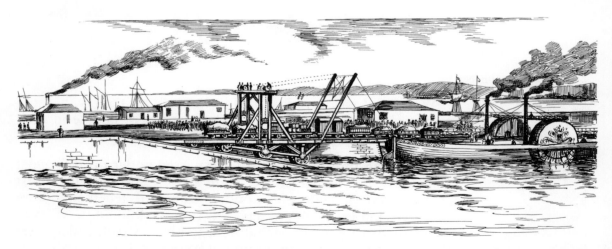

THE "LEVIATHAN" WAS THE FIRST TRAIN FERRY IN THE WORLD. It sailed from Granton to Burntisland

In 1872, the Education Act was passed which created School Boards and gave education to children of five years and upwards. There were sixteen schools with just over seven thousand children on the roll of the first Board. In the next thirty years the numbers had increased to thirty-one schools and nearly thirty-eight thousand children. Evening schools were also developed from this time and the foundation laid for the extensive educational provision in Edinburgh, from nursery school to technical college and university.

BADGE OF THE EDINBURGH SCHOOL BOARD

The foundation stone of the Royal Scottish Museum was laid by Prince Albert in 1861. Built in Italianesque style, the inside is very similar to the Crystal Palace Exhibition Hall in London. New university buildings were erected in Park Place for the medical faculty and a new Royal Infirmary was finished in 1879.

The group of buildings was completed later by the fine graduation hall donated by William McEwan, the brewer. It was also at this period that the dome was added to the Old College, with its gilded figure of youth holding aloft the torch of learning.

VICTORIAN TIMES

Edinburgh grew larger in the last quarter of the century. Between 1880 and 1890 the boundaries were extended to include all the area from Roseburn on the Water of Leith to South Morningside, Newington, Prestonfield and Willowbrae. Blackford Hill and the Braid Hills also came within the city boundary.

In the new areas villas were built for the wealthy and the middle class. The beauty of the classical line was forgotten and architecture became ornate. Terraced houses became common, many with basements or high attic floors where servants lived.

DOME OF THE UNIVERSITY, erected 1884

Furniture, too, became more decorative and ornate. The houses of the wealthy in the High Street of 1580 contained only a single chair and several chests, but the homes of Victorian Edinburgh were so crowded with settees, settles and sofas that there was often little room to move. People now spent much of their time at home, instead of going out to the taverns as before. Sunday was a dismal day when amusement was banned and children were even forbidden to play with toys.

A VICTORIAN DRAWING ROOM

Musical evenings at home were common. The whole family joined in. Visits to the theatre were made regularly. Edinburgh had several theatres, and today the remaining ones still show the ornate stucco and plaster decoration of the period. The music hall, the variety theatre and the circus provided popular entertainment.

Poetry readings and recitals in the Music Hall always attracted good audiences. Browning, Dickens, Carlyle and Tennyson all came to Edinburgh. Robert Louis Stevenson and James Barrie were among the popular authors. Edinburgh-born Conan Doyle had just created Sherlock Holmes. The young people enjoyed the tales of coral islands and courageous adventure by R. M. Ballantyne who was also born in Edinburgh.

A DINING-ROOM IN ROTHESAY TERRACE, 1884

THE SUNDIAL BUILT FOR THE INTER-
NATIONAL EXHIBITION IN THE
MEADOWS, 1886

FASHIONS IN 1872 AND 1894

Long, full skirts with lots of flounces, and the crinoline of the
1860s gave way to the bustles and frills of the 1870s. Handbags
appeared in Princes Street and fans were introduced as a result of
a new interest in Japanese art. By the end of the century skirts still
touched the ground, and the waist had become narrow. Ostrich
feathers, plumes of birds of paradise and parasols were added for
elegance. Muffs kept the hands warm.

THE ROYAL LYCEUM THEATRE

85

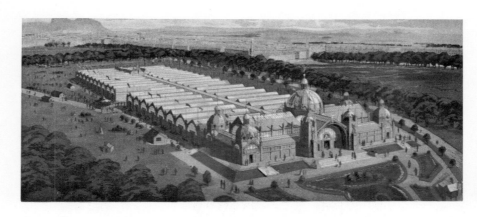

The International Exhibition in the Meadows in 1886, and another in 1890, brought trade to the city and the wider world to the notice of the citizens. Visits of the queen and royalty provided pageantry. Art exhibitions attracted many. The drawing-rooms of houses had many pictures and prints on the walls.

Band performances took place in Princes Street Gardens. The town had taken over the gardens in 1876 from the proprietors of the houses in Princes Street. Fashionable concerts took place in the Music Hall and glittering balls in the Assembly Rooms. There was much formality, even at simple dinner parties, and the classes of society kept rigidly separate.

There was still much drunkenness in the crowded closes of the old town. Tea became the drink of the upper and middle classes. Smoking became popular. Before this it was considered wrong and was actually forbidden in Princes Street Gardens.

The labouring classes worked long hours but it was also the usual thing for the businessman to return to his office after dinner. People dined much earlier in the evening, at five or six o'clock.

Street processions and military parades always attracted crowds, especially when they were accompanied by fireworks displays, bonfires or illuminations. Victories in the Napoleonic wars were usually announced by salvoes from the Castle. Many celebrations were connected with the unveiling of statues and the laying of foundation stones. In the earlier days a hanging was a source of entertainment to the crowds, but public hanging was abolished in 1864.

THE ROSS FOUNTAIN was erected in Princes Street Gardens in 1875

GOLF AT LEITH LINKS.   Kings played here   POWDERHALL—an aerial view

Golf was still played on Bruntsfield and Leith Links but new public courses had been laid out at the Braid Hills and Craigentinny. There were also several private courses in the suburbs. Croquet was popular on the lawns of mansions, and bowling greens increased in number. Lawn tennis in its present style became popular in the 1880s as also did badminton (commonly known as battledore and shuttlecock).

Cricket was probably first played in Edinburgh in 1858. Football was known, but only played for fun. Amateur athletics received additional encouragement by the formation in 1883 of the Scottish Amateur Athletic Association. Championship meetings were held at Powderhall. Highland gatherings arranged by the Highland Society began in the fifties and continued regularly into the next century.

SKATING AT DUDDINGSTON, 1838

8. EDINBURGH IN THE TWENTIETH CENTURY

ELECTRICITY, GAS AND THE MOTOR CAR

When Queen Victoria died, at the beginning of the twentieth century, people said that nothing would ever be the same again: they were right.

During the last years of the reign there were two great inventions, or discoveries, which were to change everything in a few years.

Electric lights were switched on in the streets in 1895 (although electricity had been used experimentally without success some fourteen years previously in parts of Princes Street). The demand for electric light increased so rapidly that by 1900 there were two power stations in the city.

The internal combustion engine changed transport on the streets. An exhibition of motor cars was held in 1900. The first motor bus ran from the General Post Office to Haymarket in 1898 and the Scottish Motor Traction Company, now part of Scottish Omnibuses, began operating in 1905.

PORTOBELLO BEACH AND PIER in the latter half of the nineteenth century

The city extended its boundaries again. Portobello, which began some two hundred years earlier as a few houses at the mouth of the Figgate Burn, was absorbed in 1896, along with lands at Murrayfield, Gorgie and Liberton Dams. Portobello was a favourite holiday resort. Its pier was a port of call for the pleasure steamers that plied up and down the Forth estuary. Duddingston, Restalrig and Granton were added in 1900.

Public utilities were amalgamated into joint trusts in 1888 and 1889 under the town council. The trusts looked after gas and water supplies and the Water of Leith. A great sewer was laid to take the sanitation which previously was allowed to flow into the Water of Leith, polluting it badly within the city and making it obnoxious in hot, dry weather.

TALLA RESERVOIR near the source of the River Tweed

The water supply became inadequate for the extended city, despite the addition of reservoirs in the Moorfoot Hills to those in the Pentlands. In 1905, Talla reservoir, thirty-eight miles away in the Peeblesshire hills, was opened. It satisfied the needs of the city till the middle of the century when additional supplies from the adjacent valleys were required for the greater population.

A new North Bridge was built across the Waverley Station. The great *Scotsman* building and the departmental store on the opposite side of the street followed. These buildings, although occupied at first by many tenants, were designed as palatial units adding dignity to the street.

The *Scotsman* began in 1817. From the start it was recognised as a leading newspaper.

ST BERNARD'S WELL,
WATER OF LEITH

The Zoological Gardens were opened in 1913 on the side of Corstorphine Hill. The animals are displayed in natural settings, among rocks, pools and parkland.

The Botanic Garden, which had moved to Inverleith in 1824, was developed in the twentieth century to become one of the show places of the city. The original garden was founded in 1675 as the Physic Garden, near Trinity College Church at the Nor' Loch.

IN THE ZOOLOGICAL PARK. The Children's Farm

IN THE BOTANIC GARDEN

The College of Art was opened in 1909 on the site of an old cattle market. It brought together the traditions of the Academy, the Life School, the School of Applied Art and the technical art courses of the Heriot-Watt College.

Restaurants replaced coffee houses. Hotels became bigger, more comfortable and more luxurious. Stables in the mews or narrow lanes behind the houses were converted into garages.

The trades and occupations of the people changed. In the middle of the nineteenth century there were many coach-hirers, harness-makers, japanners, livery stablemen, wheelwrights and the like. A hundred years later scarcely any remained. There were eighty-four corn merchants and dealers in 1860 but only nine in 1960.

A MEWS. Many of the old lofts have been converted into houses

Edwardian fashions for men and women were adaptations of the Victorian. Ladies were severely corseted with whalebone. Their skirts still swept the ground. Their hats were large and elaborately trimmed. Men wore narrow, uncreased trousers, high collars and large neckties, and carried a mounted walking stick or umbrella. Generally they had a gold or silver watch-chain across their waistcoats. Top-hat, morning coat and striped trousers were correct for attending church and public functions.

EDWARDIAN DRESS. This is how ladies dressed in 1903 and 1913

After an international exhibition at Saughton in 1908 several businessmen re-erected some of the buildings at the Marine Gardens at Portobello in 1910. Concert halls, pierrot shows (which were very popular up to 1914), an amusement park with a scenic railway, a sports ground and fireworks were all provided. Balloon ascents and parachute drops were a weekly entertainment. The first aeroplane flight across the Forth and back was made from the same gardens in 1911.

The First World War in 1914 startled Edinburgh as well as the rest of the country. Men of different trades and professions in the city joined the Royal Scots and other regiments.

On an April night of 1916, a German zeppelin dropped bombs which fortunately only did superficial damage to the town.

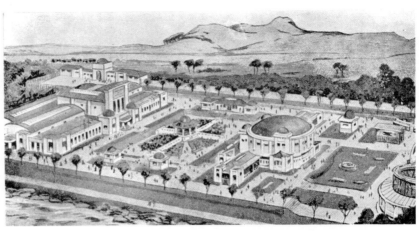

THE MARINE GARDENS

THE SHRINE IN THE SCOTTISH NATIONAL
WAR MEMORIAL AT THE CASTLE

Memorials were erected after the war. The Scottish National War Memorial is in the Castle, on the site of the old church of St Mary. Within the shrine, on the bare Castle rock, stands the casket with the names of the fallen. The casket was a gift from King George V himself. Every kind of participant in the war down to the carrier pigeons and the tunneller's friends, mice and canaries, are remembered.

The city's cenotaph is at the City Chambers. A memorial to the supreme British commander, Edinburgh-born Earl Haig, is on the Castle esplanade. A mile or so away is the Earl Haig poppy factory where many injured ex-servicemen are employed not only making poppies and wreaths for remembrance services, but also toys, household and other useful articles.

The Americans built a memorial in Princes Street Gardens showing a young, kilted soldier looking steadfastly up at the Castle. It is a reminder of the older memorial in the Calton cemetery, dedicated to the Scottish-American soldiers who fell in the American civil war. There, a negro looks up to Abraham Lincoln (the first statue of Lincoln to be erected outside America).

THE STATUE OF
EARL HAIG

THE CALL

After the war plans were made throughout the country for the rebuilding of cities and towns. Edinburgh was no exception. The town council obtained a new act of parliament by which the boundaries of the city were once more extended. The burgh of Leith amalgamated with Edinburgh after only eighty-seven years of separate existence.

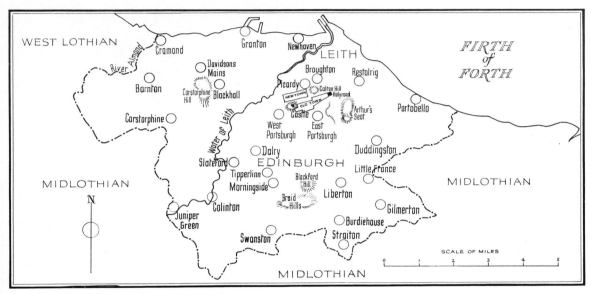

GREATER EDINBURGH showing the many villages absorbed by the city

The four parishes nearest the city in the county of Midlothian (Liberton, Colinton, Corstorphine and Cramond) were joined to the metropolis to form Greater Edinburgh. The city then stretched from the sea to the top of the nearer Pentland Hills, an area of about fifty-one square miles. This is one of the largest city areas in the country, 250 times larger than the city of Chapter I.

At the same time, the town council took over control of gas and water services and the Water of Leith. School boards were combined in an education authority but later, in 1929, education came under the town council. The powers and duties of parish councils within the city were also undertaken by the town council.

In the twenty years between the wars, Edinburgh began a large scheme of slum clearance. Whole new suburbs were built at Niddrie, Craigmillar, Royston, Pennywell and Granton.

At the same time, the city began to sprawl over the countryside. Farms within the boundaries disappeared to make way for bungalows and semi-detached houses. These new houses were mostly built of brick instead of stone. It was a time when every householder wanted a garden of his own, but this used up a lot of land.

BUNGALOW SUBURBS at Duddingston

In 1921, the cable tramway system was scrapped and electric trams were introduced. More and more motor bus routes crossed the city. People began to travel to the country by charabanc or coach instead of going by train. More people, too, owned motor cars.

With a shorter working week there was more time for recreation. Football became the most popular sport. In the public parks nearly a hundred pitches were used by amateurs and schoolboys.

Spectators crowded to see their favourite teams. The Heart of Midlothian Football Club had been founded in 1873 and their rivals, the Hibernian, two years later.

Rugby has been played in Edinburgh since the 1850s. The first international between Scotland and England was in 1871. Other games such as hockey, cricket, golf and tennis also became popular.

A HEARTS
v. HIBS
FOOTBALL
MATCH

During the First World War many women worked in factories or did other war work. They also began to play games and compete in sports. They had to change their fashions.

Trailing skirts lost their popularity, and by 1925 women were wearing knee-length skirts. Many women cut their hair short. They now drank cocktails and smoked in public. They wore silk stockings and attractive shoes. They dressed more sensibly for athletics, sport and swimming.

A FASHION GROUP OF THE 1930s
(From the catalogue of an Edinburgh store)

Men too dressed more comfortably. They preferred lounge suits to formal clothing. The sports suit and open-necked shirt were common.

This was the beginning of the jazz age and of the modern dance.

Girls now went to work in industry and commerce. Few were willing to work as servants. Smaller kitchens became popular, labour-saving devices were introduced into the home, and new houses became more easily managed.

In 1924 a broadcasting station was opened in the city. The telephone service expanded. The teleprinter found its way into Edinburgh newspaper offices and clubs.

New schools were built. The education authority opened its first nursery school in 1929. The pioneer nursery school in Scotland had been opened at Reid's Court, in the Canongate, in 1903. The idea spread but the early schools were dependent on the gifts of friends for over twenty-five years.

PERCUSSION AT GILMOUR PLACE NURSERY SCHOOL

The University erected new buildings for its science faculty at Blackford Hill. Halls of residence at Newington were built to ease the problem of student accommodation in the private houses of Marchmont and elsewhere. Most students in Edinburgh have always lived at home or in lodgings called " digs ". In the past, at a holiday called Meal Monday, in February, country students went home to replenish their supply of meal for their porridge and brose in the second half of the session.

OLD TANFIELD HALL

Since the Reformation Edinburgh has been the centre of church government. The General Assembly of the Church of Scotland met in the pre-Reformation Magdalen Chapel of the Hammermen in the Cowgate, and then in various places till it found its home at the Mound and Castlehill. The Disruption of the church took place in St Andrew's Church in 1843 and the dissenting ministers set up the Free Church in the old Tanfield Hall at Canonmills. The breach was partly healed in 1901, but in 1929 the old parish church of Scotland and the United Free Church were re-united as the Church of Scotland.

Since then the Assembly has met in the Assembly Hall each May, attended by the royal representative called the Lord High Commissioner. During his stay, he lives in the Palace of Holyroodhouse and holds state functions there.

THE KEY CEREMONY AT THE GENERAL ASSEMBLY. The Lord Provost is about to present the keys of the city which have been carried by the City Chamberlain

For the special assembly in 1960, to mark the four hundredth anniversary of the Reformation, Her Majesty The Queen attended in person.

During the assembly there is much pageantry in St Giles', on the streets and at garden and palace parties. The General Assembly is the high court of the church for the administration and inspiration of its work at home and overseas.

THE INTERIOR OF THE USHER HALL

In the mid-twenties there was a movement towards greater unity among the churches. The initial step took place in Edinburgh in 1912, when the World Council of Churches was formed as a result of meetings in the Assembly Hall.

New buildings in Edinburgh in the first half of the century included the Chapel of the Order of the Knights of the Thistle at St Giles' in 1911. This Gothic building was the first home of the order since James VII restored the nave of the Abbey for its use in 1688.

St Mary's Episcopal Cathedral, designed by Sir Gilbert Scott and begun in 1874, was finished in 1917 by the addition of the twin spires.

Andrew Usher presented the city with the concert hall which bears his name. It was his firm which created the world's first blended whisky. The old Calton Jail was removed to make way for the building of St Andrew's House, the Whitehall of Scotland. It was just ready for occupation at the outbreak of the Second World War.

Other new buildings included the Sheriff Courthouse. The site of the old one was used for the National Library of Scotland.

THE NATIONAL LIBRARY OF SCOTLAND

New schools were built, such as George Watson's College and Merchiston Castle, and new hospitals, such as the Princess Margaret Rose for cripple children and the Astley Ainslie for convalescents. Both are open-air hospitals with pavilions facing the sun.

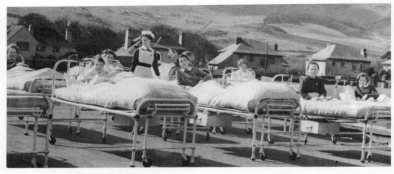

PRINCESS MARGARET ROSE HOSPITAL. Children bask in the sun

In 1939 Edinburgh, like other cities, prepared for war. Air-raid shelters were built and children were taken to the country. Business changed from peaceful to warlike tasks. Older men enrolled in what became the Home Guard and both men and women joined the air-raid precautions service.

The first enemy air attack of the war was on the Forth Bridge. The City of Edinburgh Fighter Squadron of the Royal Auxiliary Air Force claimed the first enemy aircraft shot down in Scotland.

Air raids took place at intervals during the war, but Edinburgh suffered little. The greatest damage was done to the new Leith Town Hall and adjoining buildings. In Craigiehall House just on the outskirts the surrender of the German forces in Norway was arranged at the end of the war.

The end of the war brought more change to Edinburgh. Gas and electricity passed from the control of the town council to national boards. Edinburgh protested that its undertakings were profitable to the citizens but she lost her case and her profits. The city had extended the gasworks at Granton, and had built the Portobello power station to supply light and power to the city and neighbourhood and to sell surplus to the national grid.

CRAIGIEHALL HOUSE

THE MEMORIAL SPITFIRE AT TURNHOUSE

AFTER THE SECOND WORLD WAR

Railways were nationalised and soon uneconomic services disappeared. There were over forty passenger stations in the city area in the early years of the century but most of these have been closed for many years.

ONE OF EDINBURGH'S LAST TRAMS

The last tram ran in Edinburgh in 1956 and motor buses took over the entire road transport system.

After the Second World War industry in Edinburgh changed. Edinburgh took a leading part in the electronics industry. New factories and research laboratories were built. The older industries were modernised. Engineers made power plant, ships' engines, paper-making machinery, heating and lighting equipment, scientific instruments and medical appliances. Edinburgh continued to be a centre of fine publishing, printing, bookbinding and allied trades. Rubber manufacture, which began in Edinburgh in 1856, was developed.

NEW ELECTRONIC LABORATORY AT FERRANTI'S

YOUNGER'S BREWERY, HOLYROOD

Edinburgh breweries have been famous since the twelfth century because of the excellent spring water available. Some twenty breweries make Edinburgh one of the largest centres of the industry in Britain. It is also the centre of the whisky blending industry.

Because there are so many world-famous hospitals in the city a fine chemical industry has developed, producing anaesthetics, drugs, and surgical sutures.

At Leith sulphuric acid is produced in great quantities and many kinds of fertiliser are made.

EDINBURGH
CRYSTAL

Edinburgh crystal ranks with the finest in the world. Probably the oldest sealing-wax factory in the world is in Edinburgh. Wax produced here has been used for at least two hundred years to seal nearly every document of national importance, including the Treaty of Versailles.

Rope, wire, sailcloth, glue and gelatine can all be added to the list. Edinburgh biscuits are in world demand and tea-blending has been practised on a large scale for many years.

Edinburgh is the banking centre of Scotland, and the headquarters of insurance houses. St Andrew Square, where there are many banks and insurance offices, has been called the richest square in Scotland. The oldest insurance company was one for fire formed in 1720.

Edinburgh was the birthplace of the profession of chartered accountancy. The Edinburgh society was formed in 1854, sixteen years before a similar organisation in England.

THE BANK OF SCOTLAND, The Mound

By 1942 a new harbour was completed at Leith and new flour mills built alongside. Grain is a major import. New developments include a storage installation for petroleum products, a cement silo and a fertiliser plant. Coal, beer, spirits, iron, steel, flour, paper and bricks are the chief exports, while dairy produce, fish, fruit and wood are additional imports.

Leith Nautical College, founded in 1855, was opened in its present building in 1903 to train all those required to maintain the shipping fleets at sea.

AFTER GRADUATION AT THE UNIVERSITY

Throughout its history Edinburgh has been an international city. In early times the kings encouraged foreigners to expand its trade. The trade of Leith has been with the Baltic, the Low Countries and the Mediterranean.

The University has opened its doors to more overseas students, many of them coloured, than most other universities in Britain.

Edinburgh's airport at Turnhouse, originally a flying station in the First World War, connects passengers quickly with other lands.

It was no wonder then, that in the first days of peace after the Second World War, Edinburgh decided to stage an international festival of music and the arts to which she invited the greatest orchestras, musicians and performers of the world.

THE TRAFFIC CONTROL TOWER AT TURNHOUSE

PRINCES STREET DECORATED FOR A FESTIVAL

The first festival in 1947 has been succeeded annually by bigger and better festivals each autumn. But festivals are nothing new for Edinburgh. A musical festival with an international flavour was held in the old Scottish Parliament Hall in 1815 and was able to distribute its profit of £1500, a large sum then, among various charities. A second and third, also profitable, were held in 1819 and 1824. The festivals of the twentieth century have to rely on grants from public and private sources to balance their accounts.

THE MILITARY TATTOO AT THE CASTLE

At the same time a military tattoo by Scottish Command is staged on the Castle esplanade. With the Castle itself as a backcloth it attracts many thousands of spectators each year.

Exhibitions of works of art and performances of outstanding films are also held during the festival's crowded three weeks.

Holyrood in the twentieth century has again become a royal residence. Its entrance has been enriched by the beautiful wrought-iron gates made by Scottish craftsmen, part of the memorial to King Edward VII.

Derelict and slum properties in the Royal Mile have disappeared and the ancient street has received a new dignity. The Church of St Giles, the parish church, has become in reality the national church.

A STAGE SCENE FROM THE KING'S THEATRE

Edinburgh in the second half of this century is growing upwards again. New high blocks of flats and office buildings break into the skyline. The University has built a tower for its arts faculty, and has produced a new development plan for the central area of the city. Many of the new buildings are of concrete and use the new plastics for decoration.

Small shops are disappearing. More and more multiple stores and supermarkets have been opened. The café has become the meeting-place, especially for young people. Many cinemas which attracted thousands for their weekly entertainment in the 1930s have closed. Several run games of chance but others have become stores or have even disappeared. It was in Edinburgh in 1896 that the first moving pictures were shown in Scotland less than two months after the first London display.

Despite much new building, Edinburgh has kept many open spaces as public parks. Even street corners have been planted with flowers and shrubs and are often floodlit at night.

A new foreshore promenade has been made from the city boundary at Cramond to Granton harbour and it is possible to walk much of the way along the banks of the Water of Leith within the city.

SKYSCRAPERS are rising again in Edinburgh after two or three hundred years

THE UNIVERSITY'S DAVID HUME TOWER

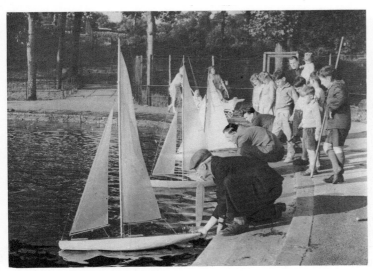

MODEL YACHTS AT INVERLEITH

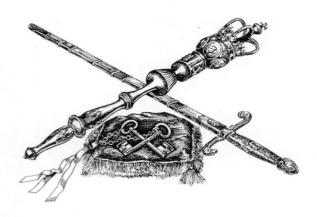

THE SWORD, MACE
AND KEYS OF THE
CITY

9. EDINBURGH—THE PAST IN THE PRESENT

The city of Edinburgh looks forward to the future. The past has been the making of the city. It impresses itself upon the citizen, not only in the buildings, streets and squares, but also in the ancient ceremonies and customs which still survive.

When the queen or her representative receives the keys of the city from the Lord Provost and magistrates, the citizen is reminded of the walls and gates of the royal burgh that were built for his protection, although there has been no gate for over two hundred years.

When the sword and mace are carried in procession they are the symbols of authority and power. They date back to the Stuart kings.

THE KNIGHTS OF THE THISTLE ENTER ST GILES'

The Scottish crown and regalia are still kept in Edinburgh Castle. The crown, made of Scottish gold, is probably the oldest crown in Europe, having been first made for Robert the Bruce. It escaped destruction at the time of Cromwell. It was carried in procession before Her Majesty the Queen when she made her state visit to Edinburgh after her coronation in London.

Under the Treaty of Union Scotland did not lose her identity as a country. The Lord Lyon King-at-Arms, supported by the heralds and pursuivants, reads royal proclamations at the Mercat Cross to the accompaniment of fanfares of trumpets. Lyon and his retinue wear their multi-coloured tabards displaying the royal arms of Scotland.

The town council also has its ceremony. Some of its members have curious offices and titles. The Lord Provost, besides being Lord Lieutenant of the county of the city, has judicial powers and the old title of Admiral of the Forth.

A PROCLAMATION AT THE MERCAT CROSS

In this last capacity Lord Provosts of the past issued the equivalent of passports to travellers. No one is sure of the origin of this office but it probably comes from the days when the royal burgh was responsible for the shipping and the trade at Leith.

Another member of the Council is Captain of the Orange Colours. It is one of his privileges, if he chooses, to ride before royal processions or the Lord Provost on ceremonial occasions, mounted on a white charger and carrying an orange flag. The banner is a replica of that of the trained bands which were instituted in 1580 for defence. Many famous men have held this office, including Adam Smith of *Wealth of Nations* fame, William Creech, the publisher, Arnot the historian, and several Lord Provosts.

A CIVIC GARDEN PARTY AT LAURISTON CASTLE WITH ROYAL SCOTTISH COUNTRY DANCERS

THE CANONGATE
TOLBOOTH

LADY STAIR'S
HOUSE

To preserve examples of her past, Edinburgh has opened four municipal museums. One of these, Huntly House, is an interesting example of house construction of the sixteenth century although it probably never had any connection with the family of Huntly. It contains a fine collection of Edinburgh and Scottish pottery, glass, pictures of old Edinburgh and trophies. It also displays the National Covenant signed at Greyfriars in 1638.

Across the road, in the Canongate Tolbooth, are charters and trade exhibits of the Canongate, while in Lady Stair's House are relics of Scott, Burns and Stevenson. The fourth city museum is the Museum of Childhood which contains a unique collection of toys and objects used by children.

The Royal Scottish Museum and the Museum of Antiquities are national rather than local museums but contain many exhibits of local interest.

There are paintings of famous Edinburgh men in the Scottish National Portrait Gallery, and statues of many of them adorn the streets, squares and gardens.

THE SIGN OF
THE MUSEUM OF
CHILDHOOD — a
unique museum
of children's toys,
books, etc.

106

A group of aristocratic men dressed in green with feathers in their caps can often be seen practising archery at Holyrood. They are the Royal Company of Archers, the Queen's Bodyguard for Scotland. This corps takes precedence over all royal guards and is present on all royal occasions. Its origin is unknown but a company of archers existed in the time of Charles II. The records of the royal company date from the time of Queen Anne. The Archers' Hall is near the Meadows.

THE ARCHERS PRACTISE AT HOLYROOD

A CITY OFFICER AND THE LORD PROVOST

The High Constables provide the guard of honour for the Lord Provost. They have long batons, wear morning coats, top hats and white gloves with black facings. This ancient body goes back to 1611 although it did not obtain its present title till 1810, after a uniformed police force was appointed.

Originally they put down lawlessness, collected taxes for the upkeep of the trained bands, billeted soldiers and prepared various lists, especially of those liable for militia duty. These duties have passed to the police, but the High Constables may still be called out by the Lord Provost and were on duty during the general strike of 1926.

Leith still has her own High Constables who were founded in 1809 to examine weights and measures, to billet soldiers and to attend executions. They now act as guard of honour for the chairman of the Leith Dock Commission. In earlier days there were High Constables of the neighbouring burghs absorbed by Edinburgh, for example, of the Canongate and Calton.

THE CAPTAIN OF ORANGE COLOURS accompanied by High Constables of Edinburgh and of Holyrood and an archer of the Queen's Bodyguard for Scotland

NEWHAVEN FISHWIVES

The High Constables of Holyrood are different. They carry out the orders of the Bailie of Holyrood. They patrol the boundaries of the Sanctuary of Holyrood. Debtors could flee there in earlier times for safety from their creditors. The beginning of Sanctuary is still marked by the letter S on the roadway at the foot of the Canongate.

The constables date back to the twelfth century and the beginnings of the abbey. They are a colourful body still seen on royal occasions, especially at garden parties. They wear light blue uniform, cut-away coat with brass buttons, white jabot, white gloves and silk hat with black cockade. Blue and white are the colours of Holyrood. Black and white are the colours of Edinburgh.

Although the old characters of Edinburgh have disappeared and the Newhaven fishwives and the street sellers have ceased to cry their wares in the streets and closes, the visitor to Edinburgh can still feel the past, even in the commercial and industrial parts of the city, for he cannot travel far out of sight of the Castle on the rock, the first Edinburgh, the Dun-edin.

EDINBURGH CASTLE from Johnston Terrace

GREYFRIARS BOBBY—the faithful dog which kept watch at his master's grave. This memorial used to be a drinking fountain, but the water was turned off in 1957

THINGS TO DO AND SEE

Now that you have read this book, you may wish to find out more about this ancient capital city. The best way is to walk the old streets and to explore the closes and alleys. Here are four excursions which will take you to many of the places mentioned. The numbers are the same as those on the map on the front end-paper.

FOUR WALKS IN EDINBURGH

1. **Begin at the Castle** and walk down the Royal Mile, stopping at the Outlook Tower (1), Gladstone's Land (2), Riddle's Court (3), Lady Stair's House (4), Heart of Midlothian (7), St Giles', Parliament Hall (8), the Mercat Cross (10), the City Chambers (11), the Tron (12), the Museum of Childhood (13), John Knox's House (14), Netherbow Port (15), Moray House (16), Canongate Tolbooth, Huntly House (17), Canongate Church (18), the Abbey Strand and Sanctuary, the Abbey and Palace of Holyroodhouse.

2. **Begin at the Mound, Princes Street,** and visit the Art Galleries (32), the Scott Monument, Register House (33), the G.P.O. (34), the North Bridge, Niddry Street, St Cecilia's Hall (21), Cowgate, High School Yards, the University, the Royal Scottish Museum (23), Heriot-Watt College (24), Greyfriars Church (25), and Greyfriars Bobby, George Heriot's School, the Royal Infirmary, Vennel and the Old City Wall (28), Grassmarket, Magdalen Chapel (26), Victoria Street, Upper Bow, to Lawnmarket and the Mound.

3. **Begin at the West End of Princes Street** and visit St Cuthbert's Church (30), Charlotte Square (41), Moray Place, the Dean Bridge (42), Ann Street, St Bernard's Crescent, the Water of Leith, St Bernard's Well, the Dean Village and mills, Belford Bridge and mill, St Mary's Cathedral, and back to the West End.

4. **Begin at the G.P.O.** (34), and visit Waterloo Place and Bridge and Calton Cemetery, St Andrew's House (35), the Royal High School, Burns Monument, climb Calton Hill to the Observatory (37), Nelson and other monuments (36), descend the other side to Royal Terrace and back to the G.P.O.

PLACES TO VISIT

If you wish to study books on Edinburgh and to learn more details about the various places, visit:

1. **The Edinburgh Room of the Public Library** with its extensive collection of books, prints, slides and maps of Edinburgh, some of which are reproduced in this book.

2. **The City Museums at Huntly House and Canongate Tolbooth** where there are models of old Edinburgh and many interesting relics like James Gillespie's snuff-mill.

3. **Lady Stair's House** with exhibits connected with Burns, Scott and Stevenson.

4. **The Scottish National Portrait Gallery** where you will see pictures of great men and women of Scotland.

INDEX

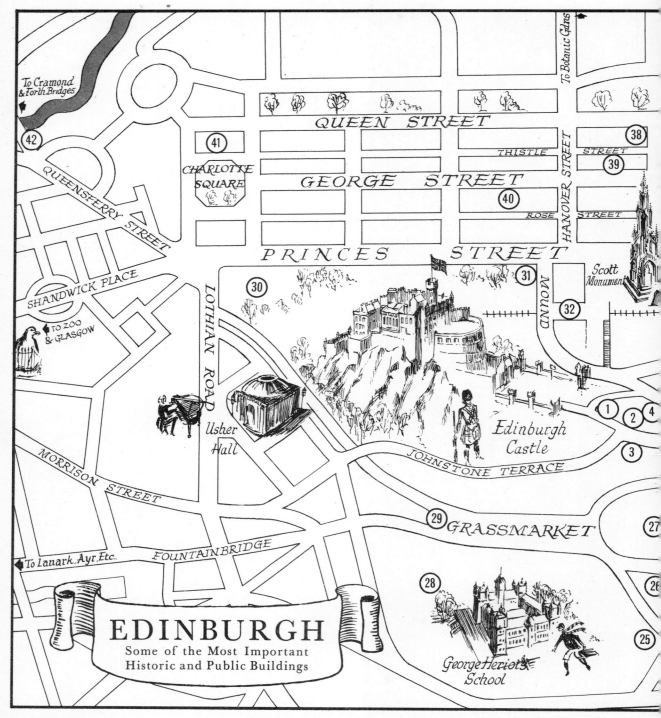

EDINBURGH
Some of the Most Important
Historic and Public Buildings

1. Outlook Tower
2. Gladstone's Land
3. Riddle's Court
4. Lady Stair's Close
5. Bank of Scotland
6. Sheriff Court
7. Heart of Midlothian

8. Parliament Hall
9. National Library
10. Mercat Cross
11. City Chambers
12. Tron Church
13. Museum of Childhood
14. John Knox's House

15. Netherbow Port
16. Moray House
17. Huntly House
18. Canongate Church
19. St Anthony's Chapel
20. Site of Blackfriars Monastery
21. St Cecilia's Hall